How to Get
VISIBILITY
In Your Organization

N PANDEY

Copyright © by N Pandey

All rights reserved. No part of this publication may be reproduced, distributed, or transmitted in any form or by any means, including photocopying, recording, or other electronic or mechanical methods, without the prior written permission of the publisher, except in the case of brief quotations embodied in critical reviews and certain other noncommercial uses permitted by copyright law.

First Edition: 2016

Please purchase only authorized editions and do not participate in or encourage electronic piracy of copyrighted materials.

ISBN: 9781078118743

ACKNOWLEDGEMENTS

Thanks to all my clients and readers. Helping you achieve what you deserve is my most satisfying reward.

This book is dedicated to my wonderful wife and my loving parents. Thank you for your patience and understanding while this book was being written.

TABLE OF CONTENTS

TABLE OF CONTENTS 5
NOTE TO READERS 10
HOW TO USE THIS BOOK 14
1- TOM WHO? 17
    Why Invisibility Is a Problem 20
    How to Fix the Problem of Invisibility 23
2- UNREGULATED CURRENCY 26
    What Is Virtual Currency? 27
    Why We Need Social Currency 29
    Why Is It Called Social 'Currency'? 33
    The Word of Caution 37
3- BUILDING YOUR NETWORK 40
    What Stops You from Being Visible? 44
    How to Build Your Strong Network 49
    Who Are Your Five Priceless Gems? 63
    The Word of Caution 66
4- WHAT SHOULD BE YOUR GOALS? 76
    What Is the Perfect Alignment? 80

How to Fix the Misalignment 84

The Word of Caution 88

5- MONEY NEVER GOES OUT OF FASHION 91

What Is Your Cost to Your Company? ...93

What Kind of Work Should You Do?......95

The Word of Caution 103

6- BEING TACTICAL, BEING STRATEGIC...........106

What Is Tactical and Strategic? 108

When to Talk Tactical and Strategic 110

A Framework to Think Tactically 113

How to Think Strategically...................125

The Word of Caution 127

7- LEARN IT TILL YOU MAKE IT........................129

The Dominant Traits of Visibles...........130

More Traits of Visibles........................133

How to Manage 48 Hours in a Day......137

The Perfect Recipe for Visibility...........141

How to Use Absence to Get Visibility ..142

How to Be Second and Be Great Too ..145

Why Decisions Change 147

How to Communicate..........................148

How to Handle Office Politics..............151

Why Staying Normal Is Important.......153

8- SHARPEN THE AXE AND MORE TRAITS.......156

Build Your Competitive Advantage 158

Protect Your Competitive Advantage..161

Increase Your Knowledge Multifold 164

How to Handle Problems.....................166

How to Stay at the Top........................167

How to Talk to Be Visible....................168

Why You Should Know Your Success...172

What Kind of Surrounding to Choose..173

The Word of Caution 174

9- COMMIT THE SIN..177

How to Build the Brand 'You' 180

How to Build Your Credibility 184

How to Do Social Selling 188

How to Get More Visibility for Less.....189

Why You Should Meet Expectations ...192

Coffee with the Big Boss......................193

How to Sell in a Team Setting..............196

Annual Appraisal for Visibility 197

- The Word of Caution 201
- 10- MOTHER'S RECIPE 204
  - To Fight or To Not Fight 205
  - No Visibility for Self-respect 208
  - You Don't Fail Until… 208
  - Learn to Let Go 209
  - What Is an Opinion? 210
  - Introspect 211
  - Three Is a Crowd—Tell Them 211
  - Don't Explain Yourself to Everyone 213
  - How to Deliver the Bad News 214
  - What's on Their Minds? 215
  - When in Crisis, Mean Business 215
  - Measure-Measure-Measure Results ... 216

NOTE TO READERS

The corporate world is not fair. While one person does all the hard work, it is someone else who enjoys the rewards and recognition. I have seen so many people struggle to get what they rightly deserve and get pushed into invisibility that I decided to address the issue head-on, and this book was born.

While there are many self-help books available that respond to some of these issues, there is not a single one that puts the problem of being invisible and not getting dues as a central idea. This book fills that gap. This book draws learning from real-life experiences, which is reflected in the organization and language used in the book. I have made a conscious choice not to make this a textbook but to base it on life's rich experiences.

This book has been written with a vast audience in mind. Each chapter starts with a simple concept and elaborates it further to address the issue in depth. Some of the recommendations in this book might seem a little aggressive to your personality, and that is okay. You need to find the level that suits you and gradually and continuously grow from there.

You might feel overwhelmed by the amount of information presented in this book, but the key is to take one small step at a time. If something does not make sense in the first read, step away and come back to the idea and relate it to the real professional situations that you have encountered. Gradually it will start making sense, and you will be able to use this book for what is supposed to be—a tool.

This book addresses various issues that impact your visibility and your position in your organization and prevents you from getting your dues. It provides practical strategies to tackle them in your day-to-day life.

The key is to put enough effort to take things to the tipping point, after which natural human instincts, both yours and of the people around you, will take over and keep the momentum going.

One thing that this book does not contain is fluff. The information is presented as it is, and no attempt is made to soften it. While I acknowledge that not all ideas are suited to everyone, this book does not aim to please everyone or redefine boundaries for anyone. If you get offended anywhere while reading this book, you probably are not ready to embark on the journey of visibility. You need to suffer a little more before you read this book!

HOW TO USE THIS BOOK

This is not just another book you read and toss aside. This book is a lifelong tool. This book is to you what a saw is to a carpenter. The better you are at using it, the better your end product will be.

Before you can start reading this book, there are a few things you need. You should have a strong desire and a solid reason to fight for your place in your organization and to get away from invisibility. Your reasons should be strong enough that you believe in them even after a tough day at work or a disagreement with your spouse. If you do not know why you want to get on this treacherous journey, you need to find that out before you can learn the strategies being taught in this book.

This book has beginner as well as advanced techniques, not necessarily in that order. It has been left that way so that it challenges you to take action. Not everybody is equally invisible. You will naturally start with techniques based on your current level of visibility in your organization and move to be visible—one step at a time.

Don't just read this book. Role-play the ideas from this book in the situations that you have been in and see how things could have ended differently had you known these tricks earlier.

Create a checklist for the ideas being recommended in this book; everyone's list will cover things that matter most to them. Make multiple copies of the checklist and use one for each week (or more if you need) to see if you followed the principles learned in this book. While you do that, come back to this book again and again—you will have to. You will not need to follow the checklist after a few weeks. Things you do will become second nature.

If you are going to practice this book any less than every day, do yourself a favor—don't read it. Save your money to complain about your sorry life over a cup of coffee with a friend or colleague.

1- TOM WHO?

On a cozy Saturday morning, I was sitting on the balcony of my house enjoying a hot cup of coffee when I saw an old friend from college, Tom, entering the driveway. I was a little surprised to see Tom that early in the day. He was not one to stop by that early for just a casual chat.

"Good morning, Tom!"
"Good morning," he replied.

I could feel a sense of urgency and uneasiness in his tone. I offered him a seat alongside me. For the next couple of minutes, no words were spoken as he continued to glance out of the balcony and into the driveway as if preparing to deliver some bad news.

"Coffee?" I asked to break the ice.

"No," he replied. "I am in a bit of a rush."

"Okay. What brings you here so early in the day?" I asked, coming straight to the point.

"I need the number of your friend from the staffing company. I need to look for a new job. They have ignored me again for the promotion and instead promoted someone who doesn't even contribute half of what I do." The pain and overwhelming emotion in his voice were hard to ignore.

I knew very well that Tom was a brilliant mind and a person dedicated to his work right from his college days, but I also knew that even then he struggled to get recognition for his work. I assumed that things would have changed by now. Sensing his frustration, I did not probe much at that moment, but I did give Tom the number of my friend from the staffing agency, and he left saying that he would call him the following Monday.

When Tom left, concerned about him, I called another friend of mine who worked in the same company as Tom did.

"Hello, Barry!"
"Good morning," he replied.

I asked if he could fill me in on Tom's situation. "Tom who?" he asked. I was taken aback with that question. I knew that both Barry and Tom have worked in the same company for a long time, and given the nature of their work and Barry's knack of making friends, I assumed that they would know each other or have at least crossed paths in all these years.

It took me a good five minutes to explain to Barry who Tom was and what he did in his department. We were able to narrow it down to three people that Barry thought might be Tom.

Why Invisibility Is a Problem

People like Tom are the most common class of individuals I have come across in the many years of my consulting career with various organizations. These are the people who will put their profession before their family, put in countless hours at the office, deliver top-notch quality work, refuse to take coffee breaks, and yet are still invisible to their bosses, peers, and management. Nobody ever bothers to stop and appreciate them for their work. Hardly anybody notices them. Their job is just assumed to be done and ready on time, because no matter what may come, it will be. This is the most taken-for-granted species in the organization.

The problem is not just limited to being invisible to your management and losing on an opportunity or two, though that should be reason enough for someone to start searching for a solution.

If we start evaluating the effects of being ignored and invisible to people around us, we will come to realize that it is not just the individual who takes the brunt of being invisible. The individual's spouse and kids suffer equally, sometimes even more, by going through the cycle of constant deprivation and neglect.

Being invisible takes you on a downward spiral, with the adverse effects compounding with every passing day. Not only does it lead to financial losses due to a missed promotion or a missed opportunity at work, but also it breaks your confidence and sometimes even takes you to the point of believing that you are a non-achiever. To compensate for that, you start putting in even more hours at work, spending late evenings and even weekends at the office, and end up spending less and less time with your family. This build-up results in stress. Stress leads to frustration. Frustration leads to anger—anger at your spouse, anger at kids, anger at a colleague. Before you know it, you are staring at financial hardships, disgruntled friends, broken marriages, and rebellious kids.

All this has to STOP!

It is your RIGHT to be recognized and rewarded for your hard work, your dedication, and your contribution to the growth of your organization, and you should do everything in your power to reclaim it.

Considering that Tom was in this situation for the hundredth time now, I knew that the problem was with the way Tom carried himself day in and day out, and the company and his bosses were only small contributors to his big problem. He allowed others to overlook him. He ignored the early signs of being invisible. HE WAS IN DENIAL.

Do you know a Tom who excels at his job yet never gets his dues and is invisible to everyone? Are you a Tom?

How to Fix the Problem of Invisibility

Good news is that there is a solution! The first step in fixing a problem is acknowledging that there is one.

How do you fix the problem of invisibility?

One way of getting temporary gratification is to be like Tom and keep changing departments within your organization or even switching jobs, only to realize that every other job you take ends up pushing you back into obscurity. A better way is to read this book cover to cover and practice it day after day and reclaim what was always yours—your position in your organization, credit for your hard work, your promotion, your family life, and above all, your pride.

So here is your chance to be someone you always wanted to be. But there is a catch. The catch is that I cannot do it for you; you will have to do it for yourself. I will arm you with all the tools and techniques that you will need. With a little effort and a lot of faith, the world is yours to claim.

The effort that you put in and the pain that you endure to follow and implement what you learn in this book will be worth every bit of it.

So, let's begin the journey to reclaim what was always ours: Our Visibility, Our Lives!

2- UNREGULATED CURRENCY

What is your net worth? No, I mean really, what is your net worth?

Before you run to email me your financial statements, let me ask you one more time and be very specific this time. What is your net worth in your organization?

Many people, when asked about their net worth start thinking of their possessions—money, real estate, stocks, bonds, etc. There is one important asset that they often miss; a virtual currency that, no matter how poor or rich you are, you are bound to have. It is a kind of a currency that you do not hold in your bank accounts, yet it is equally important. It becomes even more important than your other possessions when we are dealing with the problem of visibility.

Read on as this mystic currency unfolds!

What Is Virtual Currency?

Before we get into the specifics of this virtual currency, let's understand what virtual currency means in the context of our discussion.

"Virtual currency is defined as a type of unregulated currency, exchanged among the members of a specific community." —adapted from Wikipedia

Two key terms to note are "unregulated currency" and "specific community." The unregulated currency that we are talking about is the 'social currency,' and the "specific community" that we are dealing with is the community of the 'visibles.'

Social currency is the unregulated currency that is freely exchanged among the community of visibles to make them stronger and invincible as visibles—the people who are always being noticed by the management, the people who are always given the most important assignments, the people who are getting promoted and the people who take a fat paycheck home, all this while doing the same or similar work that you do.

In this chapter, I am going to tell you the art and science of accumulating this virtual currency that will change the way you approach your day-to-day work and will make you a frontrunner in being considered for important assignments or even promotions.

Social currency is the currency that you earn as a result of your interactions with people around you. Any conversation that you ever had, at work or socially, the talks on which you have agreed or disagreed with someone, have either made you richer in the social currency or taken away a part of it. These can be talks about a project, a design consideration at work, or even something as small as a discussion on weather, sports or politics. The goodwill that you have earned or the favors that you have done to others also gets added to your social currency. This social currency is the unregulated currency that we are talking about, and how much of that currency you own defines how visible you are.

Why We Need Social Currency

Why do we need social currency at all?

The answer is because we live in a complex world where things do not happen on its own. We are dependent on someone to do something, and that someone is dependent on someone else to do something. On a good day, most people have much more on their to-do list than they can accomplish—email to address, phone calls to attend, the report that was due yesterday, the order that was to be completed the day before or covering for a colleague who called in sick. Sound familiar?

In this complex world of interdependencies, how does social currency help?

When people can accomplish only three out of the five tasks, you want to make sure that your task is not among the last two. Social currency gives you, among many things, a chance to be considered before others.

Remember that friend who always knows where to get the last-minute tickets to the game or has a friend, who has a friend, who can take you and your family backstage for that famous play. That person, my friend, is a millionaire in virtual currency, and he is lavishly spending it on you and still earning more of it from you. Would you say no to this friend if he ever comes to you asking for a favor? Hell no!

Great talent also needs great appreciators. If you have enough social currency, it can also help you get in front of people who value talent and can see beyond petty politics. Successful people love talent and rarity and are willing to pay top dollar to own it or be associated with it. These people, who stake everything to follow their dreams, are eager to find every great talent possible, but the irony is that they will perhaps not be able to find it even if it is right under their noses. The visibles around them, who do not want them to appreciate anything better than them, will make sure that they are not able to get to you. The moment you become a threat to someone higher in office than you, you will be shunted out to do something inconsequential.

Having great talent is not enough, getting your talent in front of the right person is equally important, and social currency does that for you.

You cannot be at all places at all the times. Your social currency works for you even when you are not working by being your eyes and ears, by being your brand ambassadors and by being a vote in your favor when you need one.

More currency means more brand recognition for you. More currency means more outreach for you. More currency can help you influence more changes in your favor.

That is the power of social currency!

Since there is no limit to how much social currency you can have, you can amass as much of it as you want. The best part is that you do not have to give even a penny to Uncle Sam. You like that one, don't you?

Why Is It Called Social 'Currency'?

There is a reason why what we are discussing is called "currency." It follows the same principles of appreciation, depreciation, and compounding as a normal currency, and you need to safeguard it the same way as any other currency.

You can see the best example of compounding of social currency on professional networking websites like LinkedIn (if you are not on it yet, you should be). Through your LinkedIn account, you can reach out to your second- and third-level connections by requesting introductions from just a few hundred direct connections that you have in your network. The way compounding of social currency works is that you know a hundred people, those hundred know another hundred, and so on, extending your outreach to thousands. That is the power of compounding.

Does that mean that all those thousands of people will immediately jump to your aid, should you need it? They will probably not. There are a lot of factors that decide the quality of your network, the foremost being the quality of your first-level connections. Your pathway to thousands of connections more will depend on how well your first-level connections are connected to their first level and so on. How your first level connects with their network is not in your control, but how you connect with your first level and how many connections you have, totally is.

Now is a good time to introduce you to yet another aspect of social currency you should be wary about, which is that social currency depreciates if not used, similar to real currency. Social currencies are a two-way street—the more you give, the more you get. Once you have earned a decent amount of social currency, what you will have as a result are contacts and the ability to connect a person in need to a person in abundance. Rotate and appreciate your social currency by using it to solve people's problems, in turn making them your loyal partners. The problem can be as small as getting a last-minute conference room for someone by calling in a favor from the admin who you once helped when her car broke down. Or it can be as big as finding a job for a friend by connecting him to your boss whose assistant is about to go on an extended leave.

That is how you not only rotate and save your social currency from depreciating but also appreciate it at the same time. The more you help people, the easier it will get for you to help even more and solve bigger problems.

Once you are a rich in social currency or are close to being rich, a problem you will face is how to keep track of that currency, or in other words, are you giving enough attention to your most important connections?

The Word of Caution

If you are continuously helping people, you are already doing the best you can to rotate the currency. When people start seeing you as a problem solver, they will make efforts to stay connected with you, yet there are times when you might still miss getting in touch with some important connections for a long time. Problems cannot be the only basis for making connections, even though they create the strongest bonds. Make sure that you do not leave your important connections cold for a very long time. Remember, social currency depreciates if not used.

In this world of technology, you have many ways to track your communication with your network. Even a simple spreadsheet to track when you last connected with someone important does the trick. Once you are a pro, you will not need any spreadsheets; your brain will be the best tool. Chapter 3 will discuss in detail how to build a great network.

Once you have learned how to accumulate social currency and how to keep rotating and preventing it from depreciating, that is when you have arrived in the world of visibles! It will take some introspection, a lot of hard work, and an eye for investing yourself into the right relationships, but once you get a hang of it, the benefits are enormous.

That's that about social currency. Now you too have a free pass to the world of unregulated currency, and you are ready to be a part of the privileged community of visibles that has been using this trick for ages to rule the world.

So, what are you waiting for? Get out and get that money, honey!

3- BUILDING YOUR NETWORK

How many people do you know? Not people from the address book of your organization but rather people who you can reach out to call in favors. People who will find it worthwhile to accept your invitation for a lunch and spend time with you. People who will talk to you about their interests or about their family. People who will talk to you about life other than work and see you as a confidant.

Do you know just a few such people, or worse still, do you know just one or two people who are your gateway to the outside world?

If your answer is yes, you are in trouble. You are in deeper trouble if your answer is yes and the people you know also know just one or two people. If you have this kind of network, you have what is referred to as a line network or linear network. This is the first thing we need to fix.

Before you can embark on the journey to becoming visible, you will have to broaden your gateway to the outside world. You will have to create around you what is called a star network in the world of network topologies. Remember that networking class back in school? Who knew what was being taught about computer networks back then would become the basis of professional networking today, or is it the other way around? Regardless, don't worry, I will not ask you to take that course again. As far as getting visibility is concerned, I will tell you all you need to know about networking.

In a star network, you become the central theme of your network ecosystem. You directly connect with multiple people. You can just pick up the phone and call them. These people form your gateway to the outside world. The bigger your star network, the bigger your outreach to the outside world. The most successful people—such as business tycoons, celebrities, etc.—take their networks to a whole new level where even if they are not working, their star network is working for them.

The benefit of having the star network structure is that, for example, if Bob in Figure -1.1 falls out of your network due to a job relocation, retirement, or a professional rivalry (yes, that can happen too, you know it), you still have your way to the outside world.

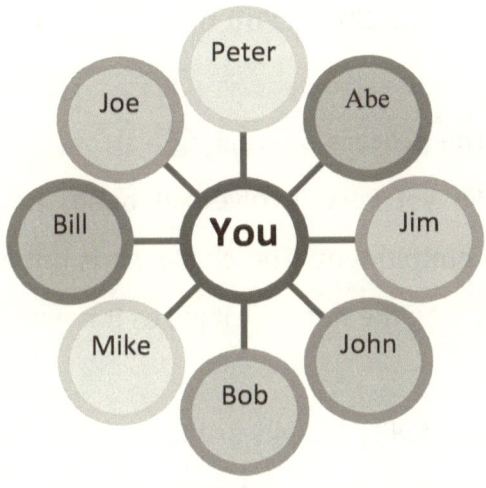

Fig 1.1. Sample Star Network

Compare this to a line network (Figure 1.2); if Bob falls out of your network for any reason, your connection to the world is broken. You will have to find another Bob to reconnect with the world again. Not an easy task!

Fig 1.2. Sample Line Network

What Stops You from Being Visible?

The process of creating a strong network is simple, yet very involved. It needs hard work and commitment. The challenge is not as much in building the network itself as it is with you.

Invisibility is awkward to invisibles, let alone the people around them. It is the natural tendency of humans to trick their brain into believing that they are not invisible. People try hard to convince themselves that they are as visible as most of the people around them, if not the best ones. To get out of the awkwardness of invisibility, they create some filler acquaintances and filler conversations.

One such filler is the comfort buddy. Comfort buddy is that one person with whom the invisibles will hang out all the time. Almost always, comfort buddy is as miserable as the invisible himself. Together these two will find reasons to convince each other why the world of visibles is not for them and how they are better off being invisibles. Can you think of a comfort buddy with whom you hang out often? The first step in embarking on the journey of being visible is to look beyond your comfort buddy and take a plunge into the world of visibles.

The other way invisibles trick their brain into believing that they are not invisibles is by clutching on to some filler conversations like greetings and one-liners.

Imagine you are in an elevator with someone you often see at work. "Good morning! How's it going"? Followed by an awkward silence for the next fifteen floors.

The only one talking now is the robotic lady announcing the floors "5th floor, 6th floor, 7th floor...." Sound familiar? Invisibles rarely get past that one-sentence greeting, but in their minds, they will believe that they have delivered the presidential address in that one line.

A big part of being visible is engaging with acquaintances, co-workers, or just about anyone with whom you might get stuck somewhere— like in an elevator. Train yourself on some neutral, non-controversial conversations on topics that apply universally to everyone, for example, weather, traffic, and sports. You can even pick a topic that you are good at; being the conversation starter gives you that flexibility too. To become visible, you need to learn the art of engaging people.

Engaging people is not just about talking about the weather and sports, in fact, other than starting the first couple of minutes of a conversation or for just a two-minute conversation in the elevator, talking about the weather, traffic, etc. are shallow conversations. You should also learn to have more engaged conversations with people. To take the conversation to the next level, you have to give them something that is of value. Share a new experience that the other person can use—a tip about a common interest, a new job opportunity, a new business idea, or maybe just a new deal at Nordstrom—anything that makes him see you as an individual who benefits him. It is not the amount of money you saved him that he will remember, but rather the association with a positive experience.

While you might wish that the complexity of the invisible's persona ends with filler acquaintances and filler conversations, there is more.

The virtual world of Internet social networking has pushed invisibles further into oblivion. While in the past a bare minimum human interaction was a living necessity, now people can spend countless hours scrolling through their social networking pages without making any emotional transactions with people, transactions that would have ultimately added to their social currency and taken them a step closer to coming out of their invisibility. These virtual networks have turned people into stalkers of sorts—see what other people are up to, envy how lucky they are, feel sorry for yourself, get out without being noticed, and repeat this several times a day. Any guesses who people are reading about most of the time on these social networking pages? The visibles. Unless you are the one who is making people come back to your social networking profile, these networks are only helping you feed the visibility of others.

How to Build Your Strong Network

Get out of hiding, get out and make friends with real people. A minute of real interaction with someone is worth more than a day of silently surfing the Internet virtual world. Go and meet them. Capture mindshare; go and be visible.

Most work environments usually provide multiple ways to get in touch with your colleagues, like phone, instant message, email, etc. There is always an advantage in meeting people face-to-face rather than calling them, instant messaging them, or emailing them. Of course, the urgency of the matter is also a consideration, but use the mode of communication in the order mentioned above as much as possible—that is, face-to-face, phone, instant message, and then e-mail. If you often work remotely, plan to meet your colleagues in person, formally or informally, at least once every couple of weeks. Once you have built a strong network, you can always use other forms of communications to keep it alive.

Whether you choose the virtual modes or the face-to-face interactions, to build a strong network you have to invest time and show genuine interest in people, their lives, their problems, etc. Consider yourself lucky if people share their personal stories with you in the very first meeting. That will almost never happen. It takes many meetings and sometimes months for people to start trusting you. But if they do, remember to care for what they are talking about—the names of the people they mention, their spouse, their kids and which grades they are in, etc. Nothing is worse than people warming up to you and you forgetting what they talked about the last time you met them. If your memory is like mine and you are bad at remembering details, go to a dollar store, get a pocket notebook and write down the details while they are still fresh in your memory, "Joe—loves hiking, two kids, elder son plays soccer, daughter loves to dance." I have never gotten more value for my dollar than what I got from buying and using that pocket notebook from the dollar store. In fact, my one-dollar pocket notebook is my ledger for millions in social currency.

Knowing people and their interests is a good start, but it's not enough. The bonds are strengthened when a casual hallway connection turns into an acquaintance and an acquaintance to a friend. There is no limit to how much effort you should put into building strong connections, but there are some minimum necessary steps that would increase your chances of creating a strong bond.

One proven way of improving your relationships with people is to be willing to help people. Nothing makes a human bond stronger than the act of helping someone in need; the bigger that need, the stronger the relationship. However, the need might not always arise, and in such cases, you have to take your relationships through a series of steps to strengthen the bond. Let's see what those steps are.

I have observed that if you are able to meet a person in three different types of settings, multiple times, it builds a solid ground for strong bonding.

The first setting in the context of our discussion is meeting at the workplace. Fortunately, you do not have to put in a lot of effort in arranging these meetings. The nature of your work should open up at least a few opportunities to meet your prospective connection in this setting.

The second setting has to be a little less formal than a workplace. Some good options for this setting are an after-work dinner or a community event, or even an out-of-office meeting with a client where there is no choice but to spend time together either to kill time between meetings or just because you have to share the same flight with someone. Depending upon how high up your target connection is in your organization, you would have to put in some effort to create this setting.

Once you have had a few meetings in the first two settings, you can take a plunge into the informal third setting. This setting should seal your bond with this connection. A word of advice: not everyone is able to get to the third setting and sometimes the relationship you build through the first two settings is good enough to get what you want out of that alliance. If this partnership is important enough that you have decided to take it to the third and informal setting, more often than not, it means building a personal connection with this person. This is when your families get to know each other, where your spouses bond over lunch or have family dinners together, or sometimes if you are lucky, your kids might play the same sport. Wouldn't that be lovely, watching the kids play and increasing your social currency, all at the same time?

If you happen to reach this third level and feel comfortable about it, this alliance generally becomes much more important than just visibility. At this level, people usually start depending and trusting each other. My advice would be to let visibility be a byproduct of such a relationship and not the basis of it.

Make the call on how much effort a particular relationship is worth and how many stages you want to take it through. Sometimes the chemistry clicks, and you might like someone as a person, and these stages would come naturally, but right now we are talking about the alliances that you need to deliberately build to enhance your visibility in the organization and where you have to make an effort to create these situations.

Easy at it may sound, it needs a lot of investment from you to take your relationship through this journey. This investment that many invisibles find taxing is the investment that separates the known from the unknown, the rewarded from the deprived and the riches from the rags. It is this one investment that most visibles learn early on in their life and then use to climb higher and higher up the corporate ladder or in life for that matter.

Because you are just starting to learn the art of being visible, I would encourage that you practice the art of building connections with anyone and everyone you come across in your organization, at least until you get the hang of it. Try to observe what people respond to well, what they like talking about and when they become comfortable confiding in you. No book in this world can teach you the art of reading humans. Everyone is different. You can only learn by experience. Of course, there are some general tips to follow that will give you a distinct advantage, and I will continue to give them to you as we move along this journey of being visible.

When you get a little proficient in reading and understanding people's behavior, you will have to focus on the relationships that matter. You will have to divide your connections into two broad categories. One is the core network—people who add the most value to your visibility. The second is the exterior network—people who can be your ambassadors and have the potential to move to your core network someday.

It is good practice to review your network from time to time to see who needs to move in and out of your core network so that you can focus your limited energy and resources in the most productive fashion. You will have to prioritize which relationships need more of your attention and time.

You might get the illusion that I am asking you to treat relationships as commodities, but depending on what phase of life you are in and what immediate problem you are trying to solve, you are already focusing on specific individuals who might be able to help you get out of that problem. This is just typical human nature. So, let me remind you again about the specific problem that we started with, the problem of not having enough visibility in your organization. We are focusing on individuals that will help eliminate that problem. It is called prioritization, not commoditization. By highlighting it here, we are just enforcing that visibles do it consciously and do it better.

Now that our moral senses are where they belong, let us come back to the topic of managing the quality of your networks by continuously reviewing the quality of your core network.

Visibles are proficient in this art. They keep their eyes and ears open to their surroundings to get insights. They are resourceful, they are friendly, they have a lot of friends, and they are willing to make more. Are all of these friends part of their core network? Definitely not, but they will not exclude anyone. So here is your clue to befriend them and be a part of their circle because they will never leave anyone out, not even you.

Easy, huh? Think again. There is no point in being just another acquaintance to them. Unless you find a way to their core network, it won't change a thing for you. Getting to their core network is an entirely different ball game.

What are those things about an individual that makes him more visible than the other? What makes people want to be an acquaintance with someone? What is it that makes them want to include someone or get included in their core network? After all, visibility is all about what others see of you.

It is said that you are who you dine with, but the problem is that you can only eat so much. Every time you eat with a wrong person, it is an opportunity lost to dine with a right one.

Business relationships are different than personal relationships, and visibles know this better than anyone else. In business relationships, you invest your time and energy in things or people that will make you look taller. Every time you waste your time and energy on a small fish, it is an opportunity lost to team up with a shark. Your stature and visibility in the organization largely depend on who you interact with as a peer. If you have a peer-to-peer relationship with influential people in the organization, you are naturally measured at par with them, even if you do not have the official title that matches with theirs. Remember we are not talking about just any relationship here; we are talking about the relationship of equals, about the relationship of being treated like a peer.

How do you build a peer-to-peer relationship with the who's who of the organization?

To make these powerful people treat you as a peer, you need more of a mental conditioning than a title. If you look around, you could find many people who can, with ease, have a casual conversation or share a light moment with people much higher up than them in the organization. These people have consciously made a peer relationship with these honchos.

The only person stopping you from building such a relationship is your mental conditioning not to do so. This is not to say that you put arms around your CEO's shoulders and start behaving like buddies. That is not what a peer-to-peer relationship is. You still have to be in the broader rules of professionalism. What building a peer-to-peer relationship takes is that you don't wear your subordinate hat the moment you see a person a couple of levels above you. If you happen to run into them in a non-formal setting or at a casual event, treat them like a normal human being with a family and kids. Contrary to what you might think, it is much easier to foster these casual relationships, which inherently translate into raising your stature and visibility in the organization.

Visibility in people's mind is also a result of three key enterprise measures. The first is how much money is tied to an individual or, in other words, the revenue he manages, the sales he influences, etc. The second is the human following he has, meaning the people who directly report to him or make up his organization. The third is, of course, with whom he mingles. For these reasons, you would always see visibles fighting to lead a bigger team or to get larger territory or to bring a project with a higher budget under their portfolio. For visibles, the motto is the bigger, the better.

Who Are Your Five Priceless Gems?

The glamour and glitz that comes with becoming visible can be blinding even to the best of characters. While you are building your core network, remember that no matter how big your network becomes, you will always need a set of key people whom you can go back to and expect impartial advice.

Five kinds of people that you should always have in your core network are:

1. a person with a sales and business development mindset;
2. a person with experience running large operations;
3. a person with a flair for research;
4. a person who can be your true critic; and
5. the most important person, yourself.

These will be your five priceless gems. You can learn valuable lessons just by being around these people.

All these people add a different and an important dimension to your network.

A person with a sales and business development mindset can teach you the skills of reading people. He can teach you what to say when you are selling yourself and when to admit that you cannot sell to someone.

A person with an operations mindset has a knack for keeping the momentum going. He can help you come up with new ways of building efficiencies in your day-to-day activities. This person is your reference for tips on how to keep your network alive and kicking or how to effectively use your twenty-four hours in a day or what you should do and what you should delegate.

A researcher is your point person for the latest around the world and around your industry. Spend at least a few hours every week around this person and let him do most of the talking.

A critic, someone who can call a spade a spade, someone who can name the elephant in the room, someone who can tell you to your face that you are wrong. This gem is rare to find, hold on to him if you find one.

Lastly and most importantly, you! You can never become anything, let alone become visible, without being friends with yourself. Trust yourself. Trust your instincts. Forgive yourself for making mistakes. I have seen so many people being harsh on themselves for something they did wrong. It doesn't need to be that way. Mistakes happen, learn from them and move on. Don't punish yourself and everyone around you for something that you cannot change.

The Word of Caution

I will not be doing my job of writing this book well enough if I do not tell you the challenges and pitfalls that you will face when you are in the process of building your network.

Some relationships are easier to build than others. While some people will open up their heart to you in the first few meetings, others will not give you a piece of their life until they see value in what you bring to the table, and rightly so. They have made significant efforts in building what you are asking them to share. Being persistent is the key. Usually, the harder it is to break into the core network of an individual, the more social currency it adds to your account.

You will have to let go of some relationships as well. After you make someone a part of your core network and you realize that this is not what you expected to get from him or her, you will gradually have to move him out of your core network and move on. This is easier said than done. Once you have invested yourself into something or someone and it does not work out, you tend to find ways to make it work. The key is to be true to yourself and not continue to put more and more time and energy into something that is not yielding what you expected it to. Can you relate this to a concept in real-world currency? "Throwing good money after bad." I told you there is a reason we call it social "currency."

Another word of caution is that when you start your journey to becoming visible, you will have your fair share of resistance from people whose turf you are encroaching. Some of them are real, capable individuals who know what they are doing. Even with all the tricks in your arsenal, you too are bound to feel threatened by someone who is a strong competitor. There is an important decision to make before you frame your strategy to deal with such a person. Do you want to compete with this person or do you want to turn him into a strong ally by joining hands with him? Is it important to outsmart him, or is it beneficial to have him standing by your side?

After careful deliberation, if you decide that you want to destroy the competition, you will have to, at a minimum, do a few things right. First and foremost, you have to make the competition redundant. You have to find out who is actually benefitting from having your competition around and what value they are getting from the competition. Once identified, you have to present yourself as a better alternative, one who provides all that your competition does and more without the upkeep that the competition requires.

The toughest fight to win is the fight of the equal or better, as they have the same tricks in their arsenal as you do. If you have tried everything and your competition is still standing tall, you will have to up your game. When you know that your opponent is equal or better than you, you have to come up with something that trumps everything in their arsenal. What is that something? That something is a cause larger than life, something that is impossible to refute. Invoke humanity, a social cause, or an irrefutable leader like Dr. Martin Luther King, Jr. or Gandhi. Make it impossible for the person taking the decision to put you second to the competition, as putting you second would mean putting these great causes and great personalities second to a petty cause. No one wants to take that chance with history. In a corporate setting, this would mean invoking your organization's mission or value statement or a threat to the organization's existence.

Anything that becomes larger than you, your competition, or the person comparing you two—something that no one can refute.

The path to visibility is a tough one. There will be a lot of battles and bruising. Keep one important lesson in mind. The victory is not always in crushing the opponent; sometimes it is also in making him your follower. When you have fully dominated a fight, and you know that there is no place for your opponent to hide, don't push him to the last corner of the world just to prove a point. Give them a saving grace, a consolation that they can hang on to. It is easier to get them on your side by losing some ground yet keeping most. By doing so, you will diminish the chances of your opponent going back with massive shame and using all his energy to get back at you at the right time. All of us can live with one less enemy, and trust me, you will have plenty of them on your way to visibility.

Another important lesson to remember is that a little mistrust is always good. No matter how close a person is to you, always keep a small element of doubt. Most of the things in this world and even in your day-to-day life, work on trust. Keeping an element of doubt helps you see things with a little more caution than you otherwise would. Sometimes this extra bit of attention turns out to be the difference between survival and destruction.

When you have painstakingly built a strong network around you, guard it with your life. Your biggest asset is the continuous flow of information from your network, and your greatest weakness is the possibility of being given the wrong information that can shatter your credibility. Kings and ministers in ancient times and visibles in today's world know this fact very well. They do everything to safeguard against this loophole. They never rely on a single source of information. Always have ways to corroborate the information with multiple sources before you decide to act on it or use it as a tool to get more visibility.

Once you have ensured that your information is credible, share your information wisely. Information is your biggest asset and a costly one too. To be able to gather a vital piece of information, you will have to spend a lot of time and energy and earn the trust of people who will then share this valuable information with you. Guard this information as if you would guard your money against thugs. In the same way thugs are eyeing for free money everywhere, there is a breed of people scouring corridors and offices in search of free vital information. Don't go on freely sharing your hard-earned information, but at the same time, do not hesitate to freely share the inconsequential information. Extra brownie points never hurt anyone.

The last pitfall that I want to talk about is having unreal expectations from your network. This is the biggest killer of all relationships. It takes a lot of effort to build a great network. You will have to learn to protect it not only from others but also from yourself. Do not hold people to unusually high standards. Some who are more invested in you than others will try hard to keep up with your expectations, but most will find solace in falling out. It is too tiresome for someone to meet unreal expectations.

If a mistake is made, give people a chance to correct it. If there is a disagreement, question the action, not the intent. If the intent is in question, it is better to step back from the relationship. Be cautious not to completely snap ties with an acquaintance, though. The moment you completely snap ties with an ally, it will convert into enmity, usually of the same proportion as the alliance was. If the relationship has to be broken, try to break it on a cordial note.

The bottom line is, have a good core network, let go of the connections that do not bring value, and be cautious of the common pitfalls along the way. This will be a lifelong cycle of network building.

4- WHAT SHOULD BE YOUR GOALS?

Where do you see yourself in one year, two years, or five years? That is an honest, familiar question you have probably been asked many times during a job interview, a promotion presentation, a career orientation, etc.

Did you ever think, why does anyone care where you want to be in a year or five?

They do so because they are trying to ascertain whether five years down the line you will be standing with your organization, meaning your aspirations align with the vision of the organization.

If you want to eradicate poverty and hunger from the world, and you are sitting for an interview with an NGO working in that field, you know you will be a top candidate for the job. Or, if you want to start a meat processing unit five years from now, and you are sitting for an interview with an animal rights organization, you know the response that you will get. I oversimplified the issue, but you get the drift.

In reality, the choice is not so straightforward and obvious. When interviewers ask your goal in a job interview or a promotion presentation, they want to see that there is an alignment between your goals and your organization's vision. This alignment alone has the potential to make you one of the most visible in your organization or make you a speck of dust—that's how important it is.

When I asked you earlier where do you see yourself in one year, two years, or five years, I should have asked you a qualifying question: Do you even think about one year, two years, or five years? I don't mean thinking about paying mortgages or a car loan or a credit card bill. I am referring to things that you aspire to do in one year, two years, and five years, things that will lead you to your ultimate destination in life—the goal of your life.

Wait! Did your eyes just glaze through that question? I wouldn't hold it against you if they did. You are not alone. Most people do not have a plan for their life; they live by the day or week or month. That is the reason most people are not at the top.

Can you live a life without having a goal? You sure can, and a lot of people do, but any guesses how would it feel at the end of the journey? It depends on your luck. It might turn out to be great, or you may end up regretting your choices. In the end, you will have neither a sense of accomplishment nor a great story to tell. It's a pretty dumb way to spend a life. Do you want to leave the fate of your life in the hands of Lady Luck? Good luck with that!

Having goals is important because it gives you a direction, it gives you a purpose in life, and it keeps you focused. But, how is your visibility in the organization dependent on your goals? The answer to that question is, it depends more on the alignment of your goals to the organizational goals.

Let's see how this alignment works.

What Is the Perfect Alignment?

A typical organization is made up of hierarchical structure, starting right from the CEO to the person working on the production line and everything in between. Though multiple organizational structures have been developed in recent times, the core essence of these structures is that they are created to support the organization's mission and vision. Do you know the mission and vision statement of your organization? If not, find it out.

In a typical organization, CXOs (generic term for CEO, CIO, CFO, etc.) with deep-rooted industry knowledge and understanding of their particular business type will decide on where they want to take their business in one year or five years or ten years. They will make sure that the vision with which the organization was built remains intact in the mid- to long-term goals that they set for the organization. These goals set the strategic direction of your organization in near to long term.

Now comes the real challenge. In an organization of hundreds of thousands of people, how do they ensure that everybody understands and aligns to their vision? They do so by the process of what is called goal setting. You might have been through the goal-setting process in your organization.

This is how it works. CXOs will translate their vision into specific goals that they want the leaders of each business unit, such as production, sales, finance and human resources, to achieve. These leaders will do the same exercise and set goals for the middle-level managers and so on until it reaches the point where, for a person on the production line, it translates into producing a pre-defined number of work-products per day.

Something that started as a vision of someone higher up in the organization is converted to a goal, and the goal, in turn, is converted to a set of measurable objectives at each level in the organization. One or more of these objectives are assigned to you as well. When you are appraised for your performance in your organization, you are measured on how well you performed the objectives assigned to you. If you extrapolate the same appraisal exercise happening to every individual in the company, you will be able to visualize that the entire evaluation process within the organization will cumulatively tell how the organization did in achieving the vision it set out to achieve.

Much like the organizational goal setting, personal goal setting also requires a lot of introspection and an understanding of one's priorities. It depends on your personal mission and vision for your life. It is not something that you can ask a friend to do for you or just copy from someone. It comes out of your needs, your values, and your and only your school of thought. It is very personal, very unique to you. It has the consideration for your family, wish for your future, a dream unfulfilled, and a burning desire to make something happen. If you have not set your life goals yet, now is the time to do it!

Would you feel better if goals that your organization gives you align with what you want to achieve in life—a match made in heaven—or if your organization gave you a set of professional goals and you have another set of goals for yourself?

If you end up with the latter, you will either live two lives, each fulfilling its own set of goals, or choose one over another, letting the other suffer. Definitely not an ideal way to lead a life and certainly not one that will leave you satisfied.

How to Fix the Misalignment

Assuming that you have identified your goals and you have a clear understanding of where you want to be in the next five years and all of the stepping stones in between, now is the time to see if there is a synergy between what you are required to do professionally and what you aspire to do personally.

If the goal that you achieve in your organization does not take you a step closer to your personal goal, visibility becomes your second priority. The first priority then is finding a job that aligns with your personal goal. Do not change your personal goal to suit your job; instead, find a place where your personal goal aligns with that of your organization. Don't just do any work; do work that matters to your organization and to you, both at the same time. That is the only way to feel content about your life. There is no fun in being visible and not being satisfied with what you do. If your personal goal does not align to the job that you do, it is time to look for something where it does.

This is one of the toughest decisions that people have to make. They are so used to living the dual life that they have been living for so many years that they are either scared at the thought of changing or, even worse, they have lost confidence that they can even achieve their goals. It doesn't have to be that way!

Depending upon how long you have been misaligned to your personal goals, you will have to prepare yourself to achieve that perfect alignment. You will have to create a clear and concise plan to transition back on track to achieve your goals, your dreams. This plan should have a clear starting point (where you are) and an end point (where you ought to be) to get back on the track of achieving the goal. It should also have the skills you need to acquire to achieve your goals, how to learn those skills, the time frame to gain those skills, and the cost to acquire those skills. It might sound daunting, but it is worth every effort that you will put into it. Some people use career coaches to get clarity in their thoughts, but if you have a clear understanding of your goals, it is possible to do it all by yourself as well. Once you have the plan ready, you start the process of executing the plan, while still continuing your current job.

Did you catch a paradox here? A while back I talked about the perils of living a dual life, and now I am asking you to live one by maintaining your current job and preparing for the change, an arguably different one. But isn't it better to live a double life for a few weeks or a few months than to live it for rest of the life?

So, now you have defined your goals, found a perfect job where the work that you do every day aligns with your personal goals, what next?

Next is getting back to the issue of visibility. There is no fun in being an invisible even in a perfect job. You will have to start converting your day-to-day work into visibility, one ounce at a time.

In organizations, your limited channel to reach the leadership is your boss—yes, the one that has horns and a demon face. But, because you now understand how the vision at the top flows down into your professional objectives and how your work is helping your boss, his boss, and ultimately your organization achieves its goals, suddenly the boss doesn't seem to look half as bad. The more you help to achieve the organization's vision, the more your bosses will be compelled to tell their bosses how great an asset you are to the organization. That is where your journey to becoming visible starts.

The Word of Caution

Organizations spend a lot of money to make sure that goals at each level are aligned to the organization's vision, but they are not always entirely successful in eliminating the ambiguity that comes from the interpretation of directions and assignment of responsibilities. This challenge calls for a caution on your part to take directions from the right person. When you are trying to do too much too soon, you sometimes get caught up in the frenzy of a wrong boss. A lot of individuals with flashy titles find it hard to define their boundaries, what they are supposed to supervise and what they are meant to stay out of. More often than not, the usual office dynamics correct these misconceptions over a period of time, but what to do if you happen to be subordinate to such a title-holder who does not understand their boundaries? What if you get instructions from people who are not supposed to instruct you on a particular matter, but they do happen to have a title that is higher than you?

Sometimes delaying the action on your part usually lets the matter resolve itself, as either the person realizes that it was not his place to ask you to do something, or the real owner of that matter will hear about the intrusion and will set it straight. In case the issue does not resolve on its own, you will have to play your best diplomacy ever to get out of this situation. Never get confrontational with the person who is overstepping. In fact, hardly ever get confrontational with anyone, let alone someone who holds a higher title than you—this is the cardinal rule of visibility. Instead, in a subtle way let the real owner know that his turf is being encroached upon and let him deal with it. Be sure not to come out as someone who starts the fire; remember diplomacy is the key.

Keep the alignment right and you will be surprised to see how much more you will achieve with only a fraction of the effort.

So, what are you waiting for? Go and score that goal for yourself.

5- MONEY NEVER GOES OUT OF FASHION

How much money did you make this year? How much money did you help your company make this year?

Two questions, one with an easy answer and the other, not so easy.

Most of us are so focused on our paychecks that we forget to assess how our work impacts our company. Worse still, we fail to take notice when that impact starts to diminish—an early sign of trouble—only to be surprised by the news of being replaced by someone or being laid off.

The truth is that we have our jobs because we are helping our company make money, and jobs in any company are only secure as long as our company stays profitable.

Our own job within the compnay is secure only if the money we help the company make, directly or indirectly, is much more than the cost that the company incurs in keeping us on the job by paying our salary, health insurance, and other perks as their employees. The larger the difference between the cost to keep us on the job and the money that we help the company make, the less likely you are to see the dreaded pink slip.

Most companies, if not all, are in the business of making money. Even the companies whose primary objective is not to make profits, need to spend every dollar wisely. In Chapter 4 we talked about how the vision of the organization cascades down as the measurable objectives to the employees. We could have created a comparable flow of how the organization decides revenue targets for a year and how that target trickles down to specific, measurable financial impacts by each employee.

What Is Your Cost to Your Company?

Everything that you do during your work hour either earns something for the company or is a cost to the company—including coffee breaks and restroom breaks. In this case, the math is simple—the greater your impact on the bottom-line, the greater your visibility in the organization, that is, if you know how to tell people what your impact is. Most people don't.

Your financial impact at your job has a direct bearing on the visibility you have in your organization. However, finding the financial implications of one's role is not a straightforward process. It is important nonetheless and should be carried out by any individual seeking visibility, no matter how involved it is.

Not all roles in an organization are money generating. Some of the roles are purely a cost to the organization, a cost that is necessary for the organization to achieve its goals. For example, managers and supervisors are examples of necessary costs to the organization. They are not directly working on the assembly line, yet they are helping oversee and streamline the process, thus saving the organization millions of dollars. Also, not all cost can be measured as an absolute monetary value. It's hard to put a price on the contribution that thought leadership brings to the organization.

These are some of the many complexities that people run into when they try to find the financial impact of their roles within the organization. Organizations try many innovative ways to associate cost and revenue values to each role and each activity that happens within the organization. How they do that is outside the scope of this book, but what we will try to understand is how it impacts your visibility in your organization.

What Kind of Work Should You Do?

Everyone who aspires to get more visibility in their organization should be able to understand the purpose of the work they are doing and the impact it has on the bottom line of their organization. They need to take a step back and figure out why this work is important to their organization, their business unit, and their department. Work is never undertaken in an organization without a reason. Sometimes the reason is to achieve tangible benefits, like making more revenue or capturing market share, while other times, it is not so tangible, like increasing the social image of the organization. In any case, there is always a purpose for all work that is done. Understanding that purpose is what sets you apart from your peers.

Whenever you are tasked to do anything, start with the big picture in mind. Which organizational objective will your work help address? Once you are able to understand the big picture, you have to start breaking that picture down into its components. How does the work done by various departments and specific people in those departments collectively achieve this objective? What are the specific activities that your team is tasked to do to meet that objective? What specific activity will you be responsible for doing? Once that determination is made, you will be able to see your role clearly in the larger scheme of things.

Daunting, as it may seem, this is the depth of the understanding that you absolutely need to have about the work that you do. This is not a choice but a must to get more visibility in your organization.

Now here comes the harsh reality. Not all elements of the bigger picture are equally important and equally visible. Some functions are more important than others.

Most work assignments have two set of features. One is the must-have features—the features that the company absolutely needs to stay competitive in business. The other is the good-to-have features—the features that are added benefits being offered to the customer. Must-haves are where the management's bigger focus is.

It's a no-brainer that the must-have features will always trump the good-to-have features. Let's understand how it impacts the person doing the work—you.

No matter how great the work is planned and thought through, there will be times where someone higher up will run short on budget, will have to cut down on the go-to-market time because a competitor is catching up fast, or will have another reason to trim down the work. If tough choices are to be made, the first features to be eliminated are the good-to-have features. In fact, the bigger the crisis, the more important the team working on must-have features becomes, the more important the individuals in that team become, and the more visible they become.

People who know the art of being visible know that they will earn more visibility by working on teams that are tasked to build must-have features. Any guesses who will be doing the good-to-have work? The invisibles, who are happy to be shuffled from one assignment to another without being noticed.

Next time you are assigned work or activity to perform, the first thing you have to determine is whether you are contributing to must-haves or good-to-haves. Are you being given a role that can become inconsequential in the face of crisis? Are you settling for that insignificant role? Avoid it like the plague. You don't want to be Mr. Invisible. After all, that is what we are here to avoid.

Even when you have picked up must-have work, not all roles within that team are equal.

In a typical team, some people are the inventors of the work product—the thought leaders or the brains behind the idea. Then there is another set of individuals who are executors—people who work with inventors, give shape to their conception and execute their ideas. There are yet a third set of people, who are the aggregators. These are the people who are record keepers. They keep track of who does what, when, etc. They aggregate the information.

Do you want to take a guess on the ease of replacement for each set of people? Yes, you are right—aggregator, executor, followed by the creator. Which one are you? The easier it is to replace someone, the easier it is to forget him.

When you are trying to get more visibility, you know where you want to be.

There is another important factor that decides how visible an individual will be by undertaking a particular work. That factor is the dollar impact of the work being done—its influence on the bottom line.

You will have to see your work in light of each of these factors. I am not asking you to always be the one who is the creator or someone who is always creating the must-haves, though it will be good if you could. I want you to make sure that you understand your work and your role in the larger scheme of things and ensure that the work you do has a significant impact on the bottom line. If it does not, try to find something that does.

Getting more visibility in the organization is not complicated. It is doing small things that matter to your organization and doing them in a way that makes you stand out from the crowd. It is being invested in the work you do and having a sense of ownership of the organization that you work for. You need to treat your company as if it were your own. Every time you have a reason to incur a corporate expense, make it as if it is coming out of your own pocket; indirectly it is. Every dollar you save is more than a dollar earned for the company if you consider the taxes that the business has to pay on every earning.

Just these small changes will do wonders to your visibility in your organization as they directly impact your influence to the company's bottom line. These are things that are easy to tell someone but will be inculcated by one in a hundred, and I am being optimistic with the numbers here.

Always be on the lookout for ways to boost your contribution to the bottom line of the company, without adding unnecessary labor to your kitty. Don't just pounce on the work the moment you get it. Understand it; ask the experts. You will be surprised how many people are willing to help you. Research the pitfalls; go to the web—all this before even you start the work.

The Word of Caution

When you happen to get a "bright idea", the usual tendency is to wait and make sure that it is worth taking to a larger audience. That is a fair approach, but once you have done your initial due diligence, you need to vet your thought process with someone independently to make sure that you are honest to your idea and that the hope of grandeur is not clouding your judgment. Not revealing what you are working on in hopes of making a grand entry means you are on your own. Discussing ideas reveal the flaws in approach at an early stage and avoid costly mistakes. You can still make a grand entry with a broader audience, but discuss ideas with learned people at an early stage.

It might seem like a lot of work initially, but a little awareness about the work that you do will save you a lot of time and heartache in the end. This little diligence will do wonders to the output of your work and help you add more to the bottom line without adding extra work for you.

When you do all this, make sure people see that. After all, visibility is all about what people see about you. Talk to people in terms of dollar impacts of your work. Let them see how you are helping your organization do what it does, but you will be only able to do that if you know what it is. Start seeing the bigger picture.

Let people understand that if they choose to ignore you, they will have to ignore the moolah that comes with you. Give them the bang for the buck and they will not dare ignore you again!

6- BEING TACTICAL, BEING STRATEGIC

Remember Tom from Chapter 1? We've had many meetings and many sessions since he walked in that morning. Last night I called him to check on him. He is doing very well at his job. Let me fill you in on what transpired in between.

After learning about Tom's situation, I inquired around from some of my friends in his company and found that Tom was going through his usual cycles of working hard and not being noticed. I called Tom and told him what I thought his real problem was and why changing his job will not help. For the years of friendship that Tom and I had and the kind of trust we have in each other, it did not take me long to get the point across. Over the next few weeks, I worked with him by pointing out what the problems were and why his efforts were not giving him the recognition they should. I took him through the same steps I am taking you through in this book. He continued in his job and is living a blissful life. He is finally able to claim the visibility that he deserved. He celebrated his promotion last week, and we had a great time at the party.

In this chapter, we are going to talk about yet another characteristic that has a great impact on visibility: when to be tactical and when to be strategic. According to Tom, this is something that has helped him the most.

What Is Tactical and Strategic?

First, let's understand what tactical and strategic mean. Our focus is not on the literal definition of these terms but on the overarching concept that will help us become more visible in our organizations. So, with the risk of not being aligned with the latest version of your favorite English dictionary, let me explain what tactical and strategic have come to mean to me and many others like me who have practiced the concepts every day to make their professional life better.

A tactical approach is focused on solving immediate pain points. For example, if you go to a doctor for severe pain, you are looking for immediate relief, not something that will ease your pain next month. But, there is one more thing that you are looking at when you are looking for immediate relief, which is immediate relief that does not impact your long-term health goals. The medicine or treatment that the doctor gives you should not be counterproductive to the long-term health goals that you have. That is when you are thinking strategic. Well, I oversimplified a bit to drive home the point, but you get the gist.

In short, you are strategic when you are thinking long term about your organization's strategic direction at work. You are tactical if you are trying to alleviate immediate pain points, yet safeguarding the long-term strategic goals.

Both qualities are equally important for you to be visible in your organization. If my life depended on choosing one over another, I would marginally tilt towards being tactical. Tactical solutions appeal to everyone because of its immediate benefits, and most people are not even capable enough to see the benefits of strategic thinking, as it lies way in the future. As long as your tactical approach aligns with your strategic thinking, you satisfy all stakeholders. People with tactical understanding will immediately relate to tactical benefits, and people with strategic understanding will appreciate your wisdom to resolve the immediate problem yet remain aligned with the strategic goals. What about people who do not understand either? Do we care?

When to Talk Tactical and Strategic

Tactical and strategic approaches resonate with people at different levels within the organization, and this should give you a clue about what you need to discuss and with whom. Notice I said, "What you need to discuss," not what you need to do. What you need to do will probably still be the same. What you talk about it and what people can understand about it will decide how much of the visibility you can claim. You do want people to see your thought process and appreciate it, don't you?

If you land a chance to explain why you did what you did, this is how you should answer it. If the target audience is policy makers, that is, people who sit higher up, decide on the vision of the company (remember, in Chapter 4 we talked about CXOs and how they decide an organization's vision), talk about how your tactical approach helps achieve the strategic vision; talk the big picture. If the target audience is policy implementers, like middle managers, floor supervisors, delivery leads, you tell them how their immediate problem is resolved by what you did. They probably will not be able to understand beyond that, and if they do, you will soon find them among the policy makers—

immediately take a note of their names in your dollar store notebook. These are the people you want to add to your core network long before reaching them requires you to make an appointment.

Whenever people embark on a journey to achieve something, they usually have a vague idea of what they want at the end. The problem is that the expectation of this 'end' is different for different people interested in the outcome. Let's take an example of a typical manufacturing setting. The expectation of end for the production line manager may be to build the product to the specification. The end for the middle-level manager may be to keep the cost in check. The end for a sales manager may be to get more market share. The end for the senior executive may be to thwart the competition. When you embark on the journey to visibility, you have to understand the 'end' that matters at each level, at least on a broader level. When you get a chance to engage with big shots, make sure that you are able to articulate the value that you provide to the 'end' that matters to them. Your tactical and strategic thinking helps you deliver the right message to your target audience. This is what will separate you from your peers.

A Framework to Think Tactically

But how do you start thinking tactically and thinking strategically and everything in between?

First, let's talk about the tactical approach to addressing the immediate pain points. As I said earlier, your ability to resolve immediate pain points wins you not only accolades but also loyal followers.

Let me introduce you to a framework for approaching the problems tactically. I have named this framework the "4D and SI" framework. It stands for D^1etach, D^2efine, D^3ata, D^4iscuss, Support and Implement. The framework needs to be followed in that specific order.

Let's understand each of the parts in the framework.

When you are presented with an immediate problem, the very first thing you need to do is D^1etach yourself from the problem. If you consider the problem and the things impacted by that problem as one big universe, you have to step out of that universe before you can even think about solving this problem to gain visibility. This is easier said than done. It needs practice and ability to put things in perspective. In an ideal situation, you will only be able to detach yourself if the problem is not impacting you personally or professionally. If the problem is affecting you directly, here are a few things that you need to do to detach yourself. Start with assessing the impact of the problem to you and try to quantify the impact of the problem as a monetary loss, time lost, or something that you value and can measure. If the measurement is getting too complicated, categorize the impact as small, medium, huge. Now comes the tough part. Prepare yourself for the loss that you might incur if you are not able to solve this problem. Live with the thought of that loss until you get comfortable with it. If after trying you are not able to let go of the idea of losing, you cannot take the driver's seat on this one. This problem has a lot of influence on you. Driving under the influence is prohibited for a reason— your ability to make the judgment is impaired. If that is the case, this is not the problem that you want to solve for visibility. There is too much at stake. Solve this one to cut your losses.

When you find a problem to which either you are not connected at all or the impact to you is something that will not completely break you, and you have decided to solve this one for visibility or, in other words, you are able to detach yourself, the next thing to do is D^{2}efine the problem. Most of us are in such a rush to jump into solving the problem the moment it is presented to us that we do not even try to fully understand it. Before you start to address the problem, you need to define what the problem is and what measurable outcome will establish that the problem has been resolved. This measurable outcome is the target that you are trying to get to when you are solving this problem.

Once you have clearly defined the problem, collect as much D³ata as you can about the problem. You are looking for two types of data: qualitative and quantitative. To obtain the quantitative information, you should start collecting statistics about the problem. This is the most painful step in the process. Most often the data about the problem is scattered across the organization, ranging from databases to spreadsheets to residing in people's mind. But if the problem is worth so much that you have decided to use it to enhance your visibility, you will have to go through this process. You will have to reach out to people impacted by the problem and interview them for the information.

Once you have collected as many data points as you can, find patterns of events in that data (e.g., happens in a particular department, occurs at the precise time of the year, happens with specific people, etc.). If the data is too complex, you might want to get help from a data analyst to decipher the patterns. This should give you valuable clues about the problem.

Next, collect as much qualitative information about the problem as you can. There are various models available that can help you gather qualitative information about the problem, such as the 5W and 1H model. The 5Ws are as follows:

1. What is the problem about?
2. When did it take place?
3. Where did it take place?
4. Who is impacted?
5. Why did it happen?

The single H stands for how did it happen or sometimes how many times did it happen. Your quantitative research should help you with some of these answers as well. Getting into the details of this model is beyond what I want to cover in this book, but a simple Internet search will tell you all that you need to know about this simple model.

We are not done on the D^3ata part yet. The previous exercise will give you a lot of information about the problem, but it will mostly be symptomatic. The next step is to churn that information to find that one key thing that you can target to resolve. That something is the cause of the problem, also known as the root cause. To get to the root cause of the problem, there are many proven models that you can use, but among the frequently used is the Ishikawa diagram or Fishbone diagram. Again the specifics of this model is outside the scope of this book, but a simple Internet search will tell you all that you need to know about this model too.

Both the models that I have mentioned are simple to learn and use. The idea here is not to introduce you to the complex problem-solving techniques but to give you a basic framework that you can learn in minimal time and apply in various settings, without needing to go back to a thousand-page manual every time you are presented with a problem.

For example, if you are with a colleague or in a meeting to discuss a problem, you can mentally navigate the discussion using 5W and 1H to gather information about the problem and Fishbone to identify the root cause of the problem. People will appreciate your clarity of thought and will see you as a problem solver, which is important if you want to increase your visibility. Ignoring problem solvers is hard for anyone.

At this point, you have detached yourself from the problem, defined the problem and collected enough data about the problem. This is the point in the 4D and SI process where you can get tunnel vision. Once you have the root cause identified, the genius in you will want to provide the solution right then and there and claim the victory. When this happens, hold your excitement, there is a lot more to be done still.

The moment you help people identify the root cause, everyone's genius will come out of the closet and start dancing on the table. That is when you lead the choir. "Let's get the ideas on the whiteboard," you say. That is the fourth D in our 4D and SI framework, D^{4}iscuss. Most people are very insecure of their positions or of being dubbed as fools. The moment they get outsmarted, they become hostile. Your objective is not to make them hostile but to make them feel that they are the ones who helped in solving the problem. Don't worry, their subconscious will continue to tell them that you are the one who helped them reach that solution, but to let the subconscious mind guide their thinking, you cannot get them to be hostile or defensive. You will have to lead them. Trust the human evolution on this one. They will eventually come through. This step is all about being a team player.

In a corporate setting, the solution or the idea needs to be sold first before it gets implemented. Nothing will frustrate you and others more than if you lead them to a particular solution but cannot get the solution implemented due to the red tape in your organization. This is where you will help the team garner Support for the idea, the fifth element of our framework.

This is the crucial step in the entire process and the one that can get you the most visibility. One tool that has come to my rescue every time I try to sell something to someone or try to get support for something is the age-old wisdom of SWOT. If you have lived in a corporate environment for some time, you would have probably heard about it. This is the point where the road to stardom becomes familiar. For those who are learning this term for the first time, SWOT is the framework where you take your solution through four different litmus tests, so to speak, to get an understanding of the legitimacy of your solution. The four tests are:

Strength of your solution

Weakness of your solution

Opportunities your solution will open up

Threats that your solution might encounter

Once you have been through the SWOT process, you will be amazed at the insights you will gain. You might even have to tweak your solution a bit in light of this new information, and that is perfectly fine. It is worth every bit to fine tune the solution now rather than regret the pitfalls later.

Armed with this solution, you are ready to go on a selling spree and gather support from whoever will approve the solution. Caution again, if many people will need to approve the solution, make sure that you take the time to walk to each one of them personally and help them understand the solution before you send that official note out asking for blessings. Tell them what is in it for them—increased revenue, the productivity of their team, or even extra visibility—everyone wants it. This is called side selling. People are more likely to approve something they understand than something that is dropped on them unexpectedly.

Once you have done everything described, you are ready to 'Implement' your solution, or let me say the solution that the team arrived "collectively." This is the last element of the framework.

There can be only one hero out of this entire problem-solving process, and that hero is YOU. People will have to accept it, provided you don't try to shove it down their throats; instead, guide them to the end, and the rest will follow.

That is the "4D and SI" framework for approaching the problems tactically: Detach, Define, Data, Discuss, Support, and Implement.

How to Think Strategically

Being tactical will help you resonate with the masses, but not with the classes. As I said earlier, both are important. You will almost always need to be strategic along with being tactical unless it is a temporary issue and not a problem that gives people sleepless nights.

To be strategic, you need to look far down the road. You will have to predict the future based on current and past incidents. This is also easier said than done. To be strategic, you will have to have a thorough understanding of your subject area. There are multiple ways you can attain this level of maturity. The most common being experience. But what if you are just starting or have never encountered a similar situation before? Find someone who has. The most unused currency in the world is free advice, but the caution is that you should know who to take it from. The biggest challenge about being strategic is that it is about the future, and no one can accurately tell what the future has in store for us. This is also the opportunity to show the way and lead. Anyone can connect the dots looking backward, but the courageous will lead through the dark. Since we are talking about visibility, this one, if done properly, can get your visibility graph soaring. Build this thought maturity while using the 4D and SI framework to solve the problem and you will be both tactical and strategic at the same time.

The Word of Caution

I would not be doing my job of writing this book well enough if I did not tell you some of the common mistakes people make in implementing this framework. These mistakes are so trivial that people make them not because of competency but because of complacency. When you have been through all the steps we talked about, you become mentally so close to the solution that it feels like you know it like the back of your hand and there is nothing that can go wrong and that is when everything goes wrong. Your final solution will never pan out the same as it was planned on paper. Be ready to improvise.

Second, do not take up problems that you are not capable of solving in the time they are expected to be resolved. There is no point in solving the problem when the entire world has already moved on. It is good to push your boundaries, but it is foolish to break your back doing that.

In a nutshell, you have to be apt at winning battles and winning wars. So listen up, soldier, get armed and get going!

7- LEARN IT TILL YOU MAKE IT

If you carefully observe some of the most visible people in your organization, you will find that they have some striking similarities in their personality traits. These common characteristics are responsible, to a great extent, for what they do and how they do it. It is this second nature that makes them highly visible in the organization.

Fortunately for us, there is some good news. Each one of us has most of the personality traits that the visibles have, though to varying extents. Most of the people that you see as highly visible are not always born with these traits dominating. They made efforts to understand what will make them visible and worked hard to make it their dominant traits. With some hard work and a little luck, you can do it too!

The Dominant Traits of Visibles

The most visible people I know are extroverts and intuitive, or at least have these traits as dominant ones. These are the people who draw their energy and inspiration from people around them. They have two mouths and one ear, well, not literally, but these are individuals who love to talk a lot but are not good listeners. If you are reading this book, chances are that this is not your dominant personality type, but you can learn to make them so by following the strategies given in this book. Keep reading.

The other trait that you will find in most visibles is that they have a keen sense of drawing the bigger picture out of the bits and pieces of information provided to them. They are able to evaluate the relative importance of the information given to them and filter out the ones that will not have a significant impact on the desired outcome and focus on the ones that will. This, combined with the trait of being an extrovert, gives visibles the advantage of talking about their understanding of an evolving situation in various settings and getting it refined with each supporting or opposing feedback they receive.

In my interaction with people who were not as visible, I found they were able to make similar determinations in regards to the problem and the solution as visibles did. But, they lacked that essential element of speaking up and discussing it with others due to the fear of being rejected or because they wanted to be just a bit more sure before they said anything. By the time they had anything to say, visibles were already miles ahead of them just because they accepted the uncertainty in the situation and decided to figure it out along the way.

If you fall into the category of people who did not speak up despite knowing the answer, you have come to the right place. This should be the easiest of all personality traits to fix.

The other hallmark characteristic of visibles is that they have the ability to take masses along with them when making a decision. They will always err on the side of the decision that will create the least conflict, even if they know that it is not the best decision. This is what makes visibles the most popular and lovable personality; in fact, this is what makes visibles visible. This is a tough call for a lot of people, especially when they are used to seeing things as right or wrong rather than best, good, and - fair. It's better to have a less-than-perfect solution that has support than a perfect solution that will get killed eventually anyway.

The other trait that the visibles have is that they enjoy the work they do. They will not take up anything that they are not able to enjoy. This one personality trait alone makes them great at what they do, even if they are not the most skilled in doing that job. Does this ring a bell? Do you enjoy the work that you do? Do you know why you do, what you do? If not, take a break and figure it out. You will appreciate that you did.

More Traits of Visibles

What I have described so far are the dominant traits of a visible person but not all of the traits. There are yet some more important characteristics you will need to learn before you can embark on the journey of being among the most visible people in your organization.

To be visible in the organization, you need to become resourceful. I have often seen intellectuals being outsmarted by resourceful people.

How do we define being resourceful?

A person becomes resourceful when he has something to offer to almost everyone. That something, more often than not, is information, no matter how small—for example, information about a process in the company, a contact in finance, that great restaurant in town, or a place to buy good quality wine. It can be even as small as providing an extra set of paper clips to someone putting together material for an important meeting or even lending this book to someone you think will benefit from reading it. That is what being resourceful means. You do not become resourceful overnight; it takes hard work and an ear for things happening around you.

One proven way of being resourceful is having more and more information about things that matter to the people around you. Having more and more connections gives you all of that. Remember our discussion on social currency from Chapter 2. The result of having more social currency is more information. Once you have eyes and ears at all of the important places within the organization, information will automatically start flowing to you.

But do remember, information sharing is a two-way street. When you seek information from someone, you should also be able to provide that person with information that is helpful to him or her, though not necessarily in the same transaction. Again it need not be the topmost secret; it can be anything useful to them, like an important position opening up in your department or a new funding decision that would create more jobs—anything that they can use. More information will result in your better positioning within your company because with all that information you are able to help more people. Remember we are still talking about visibility. Do you have a more guaranteed way of getting it?

There is one important thing about information that you should know, though. It is useless if not delivered at the right place and at the right time—not too early, not too late. If you provide it too soon, people will not realize the consequences of not having the information. If you give it too late, two things can happen:

either someone will beat you to it and take the winning credit, or it will be too late to salvage the situation, and you will be the villain who knew the answer but did not speak up. Timing is key, and visibles are great at it!

How to Manage 48 Hours in a Day

We have been talking about so many things that you should and should not do to be more visible, but with only twenty-four hours in a day, how do you do all these things and still do all your work and have time for your friends and family? How do visibles do it?

The answer to your apprehension is the age-old wisdom of time management, the skill that visibles have painfully mastered.

Start your day at least an hour early. Run through the tasks that need to be accomplished on that given day. Assign priority and allocate time for the activities that you need to get done on that day. Once you do this exercise, you will realize that you have more to do than you can possibly accomplish. Any guesses what to do next? Did I hear prioritize? Wrong. The correct answer is to eliminate.

What is the difference? Prioritizing means that sooner or later you will get to every item on your list. Elimination involves completely removing certain things from your list that are not worth your time. Do not deprioritize them, and do not save them for later—completely get rid of them. We all have things like these, both in our work and personal life. There is no rule of thumb as to how to identify such things, but trust your judgment and over time you will get better at doing it. You will be surprised to see how much garbage was being sent your way just because you never said 'no'. Once you start eliminating these wasteful tasks, gradually people will get the message that you mean business. They will find someone else to dump that garbage on.

Once you are left with your real must-do list, the next step is to identify the tasks you can delegate. One well-guarded secret about delegation is that you should not only delegate downwards, but also upwards—yes, to your boss. You will be surprised to see how much time you can save by effectively delegating certain tasks to your subordinates, peers, and bosses. Because you have already taken the effort to eliminate waste, people will be more responsive to take up the work that matters.

Now remains the work that you really have to do on your own. Before starting to work on each item from your list, take a moment to see if there is something on that list that one of your colleagues has already done in the past. Can he give you some tips so that you do not have to reinvent the wheel? You can learn from their mistakes so that you do not have to make them yourself. More often than not, this will cut the time required to complete the work by as much as half. You thought visibles had twice as many hours in their day? No, sir, no, ma'am, they do not. They use these time management tricks to find more time to do the work that gets them more visibility.

Can you imagine how much more you can achieve with all the time you have on your hands now? Every minute you save is a minute added to your day. You can choose to spend it with family, use it for self-development, or use it to expand your network. It's yours to use, so use it the way you want.

The Perfect Recipe for Visibility

If you talk to great chefs around the world and ask them what is that one essential ingredient that can make or break their recipe, a lot of them will tell you that it is salt. What is the 'salt' of the perfect recipe for visibility? What is that one trait that can make or break all your efforts to get more visibility? It is the desire to want something more than anyone else and the attitude to do whatever it takes, the fire in the belly.

Most situations that you deal with at work have more than one actor; you and the person or persons you are interacting with—the audience of your action. Together your action and the reaction to it make a transaction complete and decide whether the situation will work in your favor or against. No matter how well you plan your moves or how well you execute them, there will always be an element of your audience's reaction largely out of your control. When that part does not work the way you expected it to, you have a situation of chaos. Your ability to come out of the chaos will depend on how much fire you have in your belly to turn things around in your favor. You are not guaranteed success every single time, but you are guaranteed to leave a mark of visibility every time you give it your best shot.

How to Use Absence to Get Visibility

Visibility is not just about making your presence felt; it is also about making your absence felt. Visibles have this trait of timing their absences perfectly well. The emotion of missing something is a very strong measure of how badly you needed it. One of the biggest deterrents to your visibility is the taken-for-granted syndrome. It is when people know that no matter what may come, your work will be done. Invisibles keep on meeting this expectation again and again, and this is where a lot of them get hit by the taken-for-granted syndrome and get pushed into oblivion. Visibles, on the other hand, are anything but taken for granted. They will first create a dependency on themselves and then conspicuously disappear from the scene to let the situation bleed.

The art is not just in disappearing at the right moment but also in reappearing at the right time. They appear just in time to prevent any alternatives to them being discovered, hence creating a sense of relief for others, instead of leaving them with the feeling of triumph by having found an alternative.

The other thing that visibles do very well to make their absence felt is maintain a tactful radio silence. One common drawback with a lot of people who are invisibles is their desire to respond to a question or a concern immediately. They are so desperate to seek their one-minute claim to fame that they do not spare a moment to think about the impact or repercussion of their response. Visibles, on the other hand, do a careful assessment of what the response will do in the larger context and then decide whether to respond or not, even if they know the answer very well. They maintain a tactful radio silence on emails, messages, phone calls, or meetings on issues they do not want to be dragged into, either because it is too politically sensitive or because it does not serve their purpose of visibility. Just because you know the answer to a question does not mean that you should jump on it right away. Rest assured, there are others who know the answer too but are eagerly waiting for someone else to take the lead so that they can have the last laugh.

The corporate world is a game of chess. You have to not only plan your every move but also think about the moves that will be made against you. If no one is making a move against you, you are doing something wrong and people are just waiting for you to get buried by your own actions.

How to Be Second and Be Great Too

Visibles try to be anything but followers. They have an undying desire to be the first ones to do something. This something does not necessarily have to be an earth-shattering innovation, it can be as simple as being the first to provide a solution to a simple deadlock, like should the team have Chinese or Mexican food for lunch. Invisibles might have an opinion too, but the moment someone else takes a lead in making the decision, invisibles will either just follow or their excitement fizzles out, and they think that there is no point spelling out their choice as well, especially if it happens to be the same as the one mentioned. Visibles, on the other hand, would happily throw a twist to the option, like a specific restaurant for the choice of cuisine already made, but resist the urge to just completely follow someone else's lead.

The simple example in the previous paragraph has a message for you. Compare this thought process to a situation where you are tasked to solve a significant problem. While you are burning the midnight oil to figure out a solution and you are halfway through it, you find out that someone already had the same idea in the past, and they had already found the solution using that idea, suddenly all the enthusiasm fades away, and you are taken over by the feeling of being second. If that sounds like you, you need to train your mind to shrug off that feeling and try to reuse what is already there and perfect it in your own way. When it comes to visibility, it is important to be a part of some solution, even if it is built on a previously discussed idea, rather than to not get involved in the process at all because the notion now looks stale to you. Life is not all about being the first to get to an idea. It is five percent innovation and ninety-five percent inspiration. Only one person invented the wheel, the rest of the world is just using it. Don't hesitate to get inspired by someone else's idea.

Why Decisions Change

Have you heard this often, "I am sorry, but they have already made the decision"? Any guesses what visibles do with that answer? Don't let someone fool you by saying that the decision is already made or this is outside the process. There is no decision in this world that cannot possibly change and no process that cannot be altered with the right amount of persuasion. There is a lot of visibility to be gained out of such negotiations. In fact, some people's careers are made by either pushing a change or thwarting one. How do they decide which option to choose? They evaluate which option will get them the most visibility. They evaluate challenging which decision will get them into the good books of the powerhouses within the organization. The most important thing is that they do not have personal favorites on which decision to support or which one to oppose. They have one supreme interest: getting more visibility.

How to Communicate

Visibility is managing every small part of your professional interaction. Is your tone approval seeking or communicating? Not all interactions are made equal. The tone in which you communicate says a lot about you and also sets the stage for how people see you. If you are the kind of person who tends to be cautious so as not to rub people the wrong way, your tone, more often than not, will be approval seeking rather than communicating. Disruptive people have a knack of sensing this behavior. They will use your desire to seek everyone's approval against you and throw you off balance by simply not approving your thought process or by finding a flaw in your argument. In your desire to bring them on board, you will try to fix that flaw only to be given a new one to work on. This will continue until you are completely exhausted, or you are labeled as someone who cannot make things happen, a trait often associated with invisibles.

One way to avoid this situation is to be conscious of whether you are communicating a fact or are actually seeking approval. When you are expressing a fact or something already established, your tone should not be that of someone looking for approval, which means not using intonations that imply a question, not pausing to see if everyone is in agreement with you. The fact is open to clarifications, not approvals. Stop to take questions, not to see whether or not the heads are nodding in approval. Having the right tone is essential in your journey to visibility. Make sure you spend some time in perfecting the use of the right tone in the right setting.

When you actually need to seek approval, do not try to get it in a group setting. Individuals in the group have a tendency to gang up and sometimes settle scores with each other, making your objective secondary. Try to meet with the approvers individually or in a small harmonious group to rule out personal differences between individuals from influencing their decisions. This will not only ensure that you address the concerns of people that matter but also prevent inconsequential people from riding the bandwagon and disrupting the proceedings.

How to Handle Office Politics

Now comes the most interesting part. Who do you vote for? I am not asking if you are a Republican or a Democrat. I am talking about political powerhouses present within every organization.

Every office has politics and alliances that are made and broken every day. There are lobbyists, and there are lame ducks. There are campaigns, and there are coups.

How do you handle office politics? Did you say, "I stay away from it"? Worst answer you can give. Nobody stays away from office politics unless they are or they want to be inconsequential and invisible. Should you get dirty? No. Visibility at the cost of integrity and values is not worth it.

Like all politicians are not bad politicians, all politics is not dirty politics. Even if you do not play office politics yourself, you should know how to navigate through it. You should be able to anticipate the moves that your competition will make to get you out of that important assignment or to discredit the work that you have done. More often than not, instead of getting into an ugly fight, taking the higher moral ground backed with facts is all that it takes to thwart their move. One tip: people who play office politics move in packs. Understand the power centers and make sure you have eyes and ears on them. Learn to navigate.

Why Staying Normal Is Important

You will be amazed to know how many times I have seen people with extraordinary talent and communication making unimaginable blunders when they are just casually communicating with someone of high importance, such as their client, their bosses, or sometimes even a colleague. Performance pressure can get to even the best. The key is to minimize the performance pressure to the times when you are actually performing. If you treat every little and casual conversation as the litmus test of your abilities, you will never be able to intellectually engage in the conversation and people might consider you shallow, no matter how smart you are. Every conversation is not about your evaluation. Treat every conversation to its merit.

Now that we know what the common personality traits of visible people are, it is time to introspect.

Out of all the qualities mentioned, which do you have and which do you not have? Be honest while answering that question. These are the gaps that are holding you from being the visible person you aspire to be.

Like many other new things you will learn in this book, these traits will require persistence and patience to master. If you practice it every day, I can assure you that you will start to see the difference yourself. Considering all the pain and misery being invisible causes you and your loved ones, every effort you put in will be worth it.

You don't need to be a know-it-all person. No one can ever be. Effectively managing your work schedule and your life and effectively using the information available at your disposal shows that you have a grip on your life and gives the illusion that you "know it all." Like many other things in life, visibility is all about perception.

Being slow is okay; being steady is important. You took baby steps before you started to run. Go and take those baby steps and get ready for the marathon called life.

8- SHARPEN THE AXE AND MORE TRAITS

"Give me six hours to chop down a tree and I will spend the first four sharpening the axe." —Abraham Lincoln

I have never heard a phrase as timeless as the one above. Today, times are changing like never before. Just look around and you will see the spectrum of gadgets and the myriad of information being generated every second. Organizations are working hard to use this information to provide better services and better products to their customers, and their competition is doing the same. The one that will win the race is the one who has leadership with a better pulse of the changing environment and a workforce that is trained on the new technologies.

The pace at which technology is advancing is creating not only new opportunities for mankind but also challenges for the workforce to remain relevant with the changing times. How often do you sharpen the axe? Do you depend on your supervisor to nominate you for training, or are you continuously on the lookout for new technological, market, and regulatory trends in your industry? Do you continually upgrade your skills to match the current market needs? If not, now is the time to wake up and start doing it. This is Visibility 101.

No matter which industry you come from, always keep yourself updated on the new advancements before it becomes common knowledge. Stay ahead of the curve. It is too taxing to be continuously in catch-up mode.

Build Your Competitive Advantage

Your competitive advantage directly impacts your visibility in your organization, and your skills have a high correlation to your competitive advantage. Your competitive advantage defines your capability to accomplish your work in comparison to your peers. It tells people that you are the right person to do the job. If you are not the best person to do the job, or if your work product is the same or similar to the next person in your organization, or worse still, if it is same or similar to the person lower in designation than you, then you are redundant and replaceable. Your organization has no incentive to continue moving you up the corporate ladder. Forget about visibility, the fight is for survival here.

To build your competitive advantage, the very first thing you need to do is assess your skills versus the skills that the next person doing the same job in your organization has. Next, you have to assess your skills versus the skills that the best person doing the same job in your organization has. That is where you want to be, and that is just the beginning. Surpassing the best is the ultimate goal.

Being great at what you do is just one part of building your competitive advantage. The other part is being a rare gem in your field. If you work in an industry or technology that is niche, you automatically command a certain amount of rarity, but only if you are good at doing what you do. But, if you work in an industry that has a large supply of trained workforce, then becoming a rare gem requires effort. To be rare in such an industry, you need to invest effort in being on top of the innovation curve related to your industry, the changing laws around your industry, knowing the national and international market trends, the new technologies that are impacting your industry, and the business environment in general.

What is the latest gadget you have heard about, any gadget, not just from your industry? Did you stop by the store to feel that gadget in your hand? Did you talk to the store rep about the new features being offered and how it is different from the previous version, etc.? If not, get into the habit of exploring. Explore with intent to learn. Curiosity is the key ingredient to visibility. You need not buy the gadget, but you will be an ounce smarter than what you were when you entered that store. In the process, you will learn an important skill—to keep up with the pace at which technology is moving, even if it is not related to work. Being rare is not one action here or there, it is an attitude. You will need to practice it to make it a part of you.

Protect Your Competitive Advantage

Building your competitive advantage is the first step; protecting it is the next. If you have carefully observed any superstore that you frequent, you would have noticed that the moment a new product is launched and it becomes a hit with the customer, the aisles are flooded with imitations of the product with just slight variations. The workplace is no exception. The moment you start getting visible and successful in the organization, you will see a bunch of people imitating your style, work habits, etc. This is a big problem. If your superiors do not have an eye to differentiate the real gem from the imitation, you are out of luck. Imitators are a serious threat to your competitive advantage, and you need to watch them like a hawk.

But, all is not lost here. No matter how good an imitation is, it has its limitations—that is, it can only imitate, it can never create. The company that launched the original product in the superstore keeps ahead of imitation by launching new and improved variations of its product the moment it sees the imitators catching up.

How do you prevent yourself from being imitated? Innovate. Use your natural flare. Do the work that naturally resonates with your personality. This has been said so many times before that it has become a cliché, but trust me, you will still find more people doing the job that they do not love than you can count. This is where aligning your goals with that of your organization will pay off. Remember our discussion from Chapter 4.

Take a look around you. Who is that one person that is the go-to person for everyone in your organization when they are in trouble? Why do people reach out to him? What is so special about him? Why is that person not you?

Being irreplaceable is an important aspect of being visible. If you are used to doing run-of-the-mill tasks in your organization, no wonder people do not notice you. Everyone has limited time to socialize and hang around with people, besides doing their work. They want to spend that time with someone who will rescue them when they are in trouble. These rescuers are 'irreplaceable' in the organization. Things that make a person irreplaceable are knowledge about their work, experience in their field, and their familiarity with the environment. That is what sharpening the axe means. It means remaining relevant to the work that you do.

All these things combined decide your competitive advantage, which in turn determine your position, your status, and even your perks in your company. Your competitive advantage makes people see you as a problem solver. Keep in mind, no matter how good you are at what you do, there will always be certain things that will be new to you, things that will be thrown to you and you will be required to provide a solution or an opinion on them.

Increase Your Knowledge Multifold

There are so many situations that a professional might run into that experiencing all of them personally will take a lifetime or more. If you have to provide a solution to an entirely new problem that you have not seen in the past, you need to be able to draw from the experience of the masses. That is when being associated with professional organizations comes in handy. Some of the popular ones that you might have heard of are pmi.org, toastmaster.org, and IEEE.org. Of course, you will have to choose the ones that are relevant to your field.

Just paying the membership fees to these organizations is not going to do any good. You have to be actively involved in the regular functioning of these organizations. You will have to get involved with their local chapters, go for networking dinners, share your experiences and learn from the experiences of others. Your membership earns you access to high-quality information and collective experience of hundreds of members of the organization. These professional associations can help you deliver a proven solution to a problem. You can learn from the collective experience of the group rather than trying to solve a mammoth problem alone. In fact, you don't have to wait for a problem to tap into the rich knowledge of a professional association; these association members meet regularly to discuss industry trends, challenges faced, and the solutions that worked. Participating in these discussions adds to your competitive advantage. When you start engaging in these discussions regularly is when you have made building your competitive advantage your habit. Considering the wealth of information that you get out of such organizations, your membership fee is worth every penny.

How to Handle Problems

Being proactive is also the second nature of the visible. Do not wait for things to reach you. Be proactive and reach out to the problems before they reach you. This is counterintuitive to our fundamental nature. As human beings, we are conditioned to stay as far as possible from the problems, and that is the reason we wait for a problem to come to us, and reluctantly, after we have tried everything to deflect it, we think about solving it. Change that behavior; attack the problem before it attacks you.

How to Stay at the Top

If you are disciplined and a hard worker, with some luck, you should be able to make it to the top of the corporate ladder, staying at the top, however, is what most invisibles struggle with. Once you reach the top, you need very specific skills to stay there. When you reach the top, you get the authority by default, but if that is all that you have, nothing is stopping you from being replaced one day.

What is, then, that perfect sauce to stay at the helm? It is by being abreast of the tricks of the trade, changing your outlook from managing transactions to setting direction, and continuously updating your knowledge about your industry. Knowledge always trumps authority. Authority is respected only in a particular setting, knowledge is respected everywhere. The perfect recipe for staying at the top is finding that delicate balance between use of knowledge and use of power. When in doubt, err on the side of knowledge.

How to Talk to Be Visible

Effective and crisp communication, clear pronunciation and a clearly audible voice are a must to become visible. Do you often find yourself providing suggestions to the person sitting next to you in the meeting room rather than to the entire group? Do you find that whenever you speak to address the group, people have already moved on to the next topic? Never be afraid of sharing your ideas. Even if an idea is wrong, you will still eliminate one possible wrong solution and bring your team that much closer to finding the right one. Thomas Edison made over a thousand unsuccessful attempts at inventing the light bulb before he could get it working. In fact, more often than not, a wrong solution is the one that leads to a right solution. Your wrong solution might just be the spark that was needed to guide the team in the right direction. Say it, and say it with authority. There is no harm in starting with, "I have a suggestion. I'm not sure if it will solve the problem, but I want to put it on the table."

You will be surprised at how many people will be willing to swap places with you just to be able to make that statement. You should know that when you decided to speak, you were among the very few in that meeting group that had anything to contribute at all, most of them were there because they could not skip the meeting, possibly because their boss was in that meeting or they did not have any other place to be.

The other reason why most people do not speak up is that they do not have enough background about the topic to even start analyzing it, and that is because they never did their homework before coming to the meeting. Never go unprepared to a meeting or anywhere that requires people to collectively resolve a situation. Do not think that someone else will have the solution. Always prepare as if you are the only one who will have to herd the cats. It is okay to be wrong, it is a crime to be unprepared.

Sometimes speaking up is the only difference between being invisible and being visible. When you speak, though, keep in mind that it is not what you say that matters; it is what the audience hears that matters.

Talk in a language that makes people comfortable and makes it easier for them to follow you. Know your audience. If you are talking to the senior executives in your company and you start telling them the highly technical architecture of the new circuit board that you designed, you have lost them in first thirty seconds. Those poor guys only wanted to know if there is a market out there for such circuits. *I can't stress this enough—know your audience before you decide what to speak.*

Why You Should Know Your Success

A lot has been written about analyzing your mistakes and why something did not work. But seldom will you find people telling you to analyze your success and see why something worked. When you try your hand at something new, you will try different things to see what works, changing your approach many times along on the way. While you are doing all that, keep in mind that whenever and however you hit the finish mark, people will expect you to be able to do it again when needed. If you are among the few who don't remember how they got there, you are in big trouble. Knowing why things worked is equally important as knowing why they did not. If you don't know why it worked, you might not be able to make it work again. You will end up being labeled as yet another first-time lucky person. Analyze your success as much as or more than you would analyze your failure. There are twice as many insecure people ready to take down a one-time successful man than there are for a failed one.

What Kind of Surrounding to Choose

Becoming visible and getting dues for our work is our ultimate goal, but it is also important to be cognizant of the environment you are trying to achieve this in. Getting rewarded is an intrinsic human desire. People, no matter how high up, have a desire to be appreciated and rewarded for what they do, and this is the core human trait that management across the world uses to drive people to act in certain ways or to demonstrate particular behaviors. Since the effect of rewards and appreciation has such an enormous impact on anyone, you should carefully choose the environment that you compete in. Evaluate what kind of behavior is rewarded and make sure that it aligns with your value system. Stay away from an environment where mediocrity and sycophancy are rewarded. If you don't get out of such a system soon enough, your intrinsic desire to be rewarded will force you to adapt to the environment. Before you realize it, mediocrity and sycophancy will become your second nature. Therefore, compete in an environment where excellence is rewarded. There is no fun in being the most visible person among a bunch of scumbags.

The Word of Caution

While we are talking about sharpening old skills and acquiring new ones, I should also warn you about the uphill task ahead of you. You always hear people talking about successful people and how they want to be in their place. Needless to say, there is more to success than what meets the eye. Preceding success is tremendously hard work, disappointments, failures, and mockeries. Like success, ultimate visibility is also cherished by many, if not all. The path to visibility, like success, has to go through failure and mediocrity. You will need to weather the mediocrity before you can be great. The thing that keeps the visibles going through this phase is the reward of visibility at the end, and it should keep you going too. Have comfort in the fact that most visibles that you see out there have been through the same treacherous journey that you are going through today. The reward at the end is worth every pain that you have to bear. If you give up halfway, the burden of the loss is yours to carry.

As we conclude this discussion, I should reiterate, don't try to be a know-it-all person. Be aware of your weaknesses. Find ways to fix them, if you can, but also be mindful of the fact that you won't be able to fix all of them. Learn to work with the ones that you cannot fix. If I don't know how to swim, I don't jump in the ocean. If you are not much of a casual talker, like me, and you have to meet a chatty client, take a crutch with you, someone who can talk. The bottom line is, learn as many skills as you humanly can and use your network to compensate for ones that you cannot.

Here is a little secret for you, Einstein was a genius, others are just a bit better prepared than you are. Go out and bring the 'genius' in you alive.

9- COMMIT THE SIN

All the talent that you have is only useful if you can get it in front of the right audience.

There is nothing more common in this world than a talented person with no stage to showcase his talent. This is not without reason. Learning and mastering a new skill is not easy, and if you add another trait to the mix—the art to sell that skill—it becomes an uphill task for any mortal. It is not a surprise that the finest art is often found on the streets. Lucky are the ones who get discovered by people with a taste for talent and the skill for selling. They go on to become world famous personalities.

The moral is that talent alone is not enough to make you visible if you don't know how to sell it or don't have someone who can sell it for you.

For most people who are not in the business of selling, selling seems to be a forbidden thing. Every time we think of selling, we are reminded of that pushy salesman who tries hard to make us believe that buying his product is the only purpose for which we were born.

Visibles, however, will sell at any and all opportunity they get, and they sell just one thing—themselves. They miss no chance of telling people, directly or through someone else, how they helped save that distressed project or how they bagged that tough client or how they burned the midnight oil to meet that deadline.

You did all this too, but did you sell it? Why not?

Whether you realize it or not, the reality is that we all are selling something. Someone is selling a great idea to the management, or someone else is selling the request to take time off. Anytime you need to get anyone on board to your train of thought, you are selling, be it at work or in your personal life. The problem arises when you try too hard not to make that selling look obvious, and you get caught up between doing and not doing enough and end up selling yourself short. The end result is that you do not get the recognition you deserve; worse still, someone else gets it just because they sold it right. This leaves you disappointed; disappointment pushes you into hiding, and you end up cursing the world for not being fair, and the dreaded invisibility glooms.

How to Build the Brand 'You'

The mantra of being visible is that you have to build the brand 'you'. So far we have learned how to strengthen the product 'you'—a product that is skilled, a product that understands business value, a product that loves what he does, and a product that continuously improves. Once the product 'you' is ready, brand 'you' needs to follow. To create that brand, you need to sell the product 'you'.

My intent here is not to convert you into that annoying salesman but to give you some ideas on how to get credit for the work that you have done and to help you get what you deserve.

You do not need to be the best product out there; you just need to be good enough. Being best is an illusion; being good is the reality. You need to keep getting better at being good, every day.

In the same way that beauty lies in the eyes of the beholder, considering something good or not good lies in the mind of your audience; it is a matter of their perception. Something that is of exceptional quality to one might be junk to someone else. Something that you thought was top notch is thrown out in no time, and you are left wondering what just happened. This happens every day, even to the very best.

If quality were that subjective, wouldn't it make sense to know what quality means to the audience that is ultimately going to judge the product 'you'? It's a simple idea but often overlooked. Before you embark on the journey to accomplish something, make sure you understand what is expected of you to avoid any disappointment later. You don't have to be the best, but you have to be the best by the definition of the person who matters.

Be mindful, though, no amount of selling can make an inferior product shine. You might be able to create momentary illusions of excellence, but before you know it, it will fade away. So, before you build a brand 'you', work hard on honing the product 'you'. You will find a few undeserving people who will somehow make their way up in the organization, making you wonder if investing time and effort in keeping yourself competitive is even worth it. The only answer to that is, 'yes, it is worth every effort'.

Getting visibility is not a one-time earn-and-done deal, and it definitely is not something that should require you to schmooze with someone. The difference between your visibility and the visibility of an undeserving person should be the sustainability of it. An undeserving person has to be spineless and has to rely on deceit and flattery to be able to beg his visibility. Such a person is always at the mercy of his master to be able to maintain his stature in the organization. A person whose visibility is backed by merit commands the visibility. His visibility, once earned, is invincible, and he is then not dependent on a particular individual or group of individuals to continue being visible. He is armed with tactics to maneuver his way to visibility, but he earns his visibility as he moves along the way. His skill is in getting himself in front of the right audience who will then bow to his talent and not just bestow upon him the visibility for any reason other than his merit.

How to Build Your Credibility

If you talk to any good salesman, there is one thing that they will tell you: the biggest sales in the world happen on credibility first and product second. While having a great product 'you' is imperative, you should also have the credibility among your colleagues before you can start selling the brand 'you'. While there are many ways to build credibility, living up to your commitments tops the list. If you tell someone that you will do something, make sure that you do it. If you are not able to, let them know that you can't. People are more forgiving of someone's inability to fulfill an obligation than of being kept in the dark.

Getting credentialed is also an excellent way to add credibility to brand 'you.' There are professional bodies in every field, which provide accreditations to professionals working in that area. Once you are credentialed, it is easier for people to believe that you have at the least the fundamental understanding of your field. It will not establish you as an expert, but it will give people a reason to give you a chance to prove that you are one.

Another way to get credibility in your workplace is to get credible people to endorse you. Endorsements are always a safer bet than you trying to tell someone about your contribution to a particular task. There is a fine line between highlighting your contribution and bragging. Crossing this line can be counterproductive to your objective. Endorsements are a great way to stay on the right side of that line. Endorsements can come from anyone, including a customer, your supervisor, or even a colleague. All endorsements are good endorsements, no matter how small. If people forget to give them on their own, there is no shame in asking for it, but only after you have earned it. Having to ask for endorsements does two good things. First, it makes you think twice about your role in the situation before you go and ask for that extra credit. Second, once you have done the first step, it gives you that extra ounce of confidence needed to demand that honorary mention.

Whenever you request an endorsement, ask the endorser to state what the situation was, what the solution was, how the team worked together to come to a solution, and how your knowledge of something very specific helped the team fine tune the solution or save those extra hours of work. With this level of detail, you can rest assured that the endorsement will be fairly received by everyone.

Helping others and sharing your knowledge are the best forms of selling. People never forget someone who has helped them in a time of need and will go out of their way to acknowledge your contributions and to endorse you, sometimes even before you ask for it. Remember, more endorsement is more visibility.

If you are just starting to build your credibility or if you find it difficult to directly ask for an endorsement, start in a subtle way by requesting feedback for your work instead of an endorsement. People are more forthcoming to provide feedback than a direct endorsement to someone whom they have not known for long. It gives you not only an independent review of your work but also an opportunity to make amends in case the feedback is not positive and before it becomes a general opinion.

How to Do Social Selling

Social selling is also a great way to add volumes to your visibility. When I talk about social selling, I am referring to virtual web networks as well as local social networks, where you can meet people face to face. The great thing about social selling is that it has not only a vast outreach for a small portion of time that you spend but also an outreach to the who's who of your industry. Most social groups have simple membership requirements, and it is not uncommon for people to share such a social group with someone much higher up in their organization. Just compare this with the effort it will take to have your reputation reach the executives within your organization using your normal official channels.

There are proven ways of selling brand 'you' in these social settings. Find your strengths related to your business, market trends, or anything that you are good at—work related or outside. Join local groups that share the same interests as yours. Share knowledge, participate in events, more importantly, have fun around people who think like you. You will be surprised to see how the graph of your visibility skyrockets. Take the same behavior to online forums. Participate in online forums and discussions around your area of expertise. Let the world know your metal.

How to Get More Visibility for Less

Visibility is a costly proposition. The amount of effort that you put in to get an ounce of visibility is extraordinary, especially when you are just getting started on the journey to becoming visible. Of course, it is all worth it, that is why we all are here.

There are some opportunities in a regular work setting where you can get significant visibility by putting in much less effort, like team-building exercises, team outings, and office parties. Most of these events happen in a semi-formal environment that gives people an opportunity to showcase a different side of their personality that usually does not come out in a formal setting. Try to use any of your outside-work skills to earn some visibility points. This outside-work skill can be anything from arranging a small game or a quiz at the event to helping with icebreakers and making sure that everyone is engaged in the event. Make sure to casually remind people of your name and department at least a few times in the process, after all, that's what we want people to remember: *'If anyone needs a bingo ticket or a pen, call for Joe from finance.'* People are more likely to remember your name and the face from an entertaining event than a boring meeting.

Your company's intranet is another way of reaching out to people. When you visit the intranet of your company, you see news, articles, guest blogs, etc. Who do you think writes all that content? It is people who have a keen desire to build an outreach and to share their knowledge with fellow workers. Have you ever tried to publish something on the intranet, something that will benefit others? If there is one medium of creating a brand 'you' in your organization that is severely underused, it is your company's intranet and knowledge forums. Make sure you get the most out of it. It is a free and powerful outreach, but only if you have something valuable to share.

Why You Should Meet Expectations

If you do what is being asked of you and if you are any good at what you do, sooner or later you will catch the eye of someone important. Intellectuals have a knack for being connected. Good word travels faster than you think. You will be surprised to see how quickly your name reaches someone higher up in your organization. Once they know your worth, they will not waste a minute in getting in touch with you, and that is what makes them elite. If they reach out to you, it will be most likely to discuss an idea they are working on or a challenge they are facing. Something they think you might be able to help with. Mind you, most of these people are very passionate about what they do, and they are deeply invested in their ideas and problems. If they happen to see a savior in you, make sure you live up to their expectations, even if it means burning the midnight oil and putting in some extra effort. Opportunities like these don't come every day, but if they do, make sure that you get the most out of them. Remember, the higher you are connected, the more you are visible.

Coffee with the Big Boss

There is another rather unusual medium to catch the eye of executives. You might have seen this medium being used a dozen times but were too naïve to understand what actually was happening. That medium is the company elevator, the office cafeteria, or even the coffee machines. These places have a unique atmosphere around them. In those locations, people are in their official mindset, yet open to engaging in light conversation. This is where you have an opportunity to engage with executives in an intellectual conversation, a conversation that matters to them. Notice I mentioned 'conversation that matters to them,' which means that it might be a casual break for them, but a much-awaited encounter for you.

You are free to have a casual conversation with anyone, but when you find an important executive in a setting where you can slip in a conversation, you do not want to waste it talking about something that he will forget the moment he walks away. These chance encounters are not to be wasted in talking about the game last night or the weather next week. You will have to make sure that you have done your homework on that executive and what matters to him. Remember, it is a casual encounter for him but not for you. Be ready for what is called a thirty-second elevator pitch in the sales world. Thirty seconds of what matters to him. That is all the time you are going to get from him. Keep in mind the key is to slip in a conversation casually, not to hard sell.

I must warn you about selling to executives. When your visibility is half-baked, it is tempting to get carried away and drop your guard. When your plan to get more and more visibility starts working, you will have a lot of casual off-work kind of conversations with people in power. Until you have totally understood the nature of the individual, do not be anything less than a thorough professional, even in your casual conversations. Just because someone has been smiling and has been nice to you in a conversation is no reason to believe that you can get ultra-casual with them right away, though that is where you want to ultimately take the relationship to get the most benefit from that alliance. The key is to take it slow and give yourself enough time to read the dynamics of an evolving relationship.

How to Sell in a Team Setting

Selling brand 'you' is a continuous process, though it becomes a little tricky if you work in an environment where teams, and not individuals, are assigned a goal. Most people find it tough to credit the success to an individual if many people were involved in accomplishing the work, even if those people have made varying degrees of contributions. This is just human nature. Failures are a different story, though. Visibles know this very well. They guide people, sometimes in a very subtle way, to reach a conclusion that they were the primary drivers of success. They don't have to claim the victory right then and there, they just have to plant that seed in their mind and reinforce it time and again—human psychology will do the rest. Remember that MVP award winner from your team that left you wondering what he did differently than anyone else on the team? He did a good job selling!

Selling in a team setting just reinforces the fact that highlighting your role in getting past a difficult problem or even in an ordinary course of execution of the work need not wait until the work completes; it needs to happen on an ongoing basis.

Annual Appraisal for Visibility

There is another massive yet most neglected opportunity when you get to sell the brand 'you'—a time when you have the undivided attention of your boss, a time when your boss is paid and mandated to hear your selling pitch. It is the time when you have to present the summary of your accomplishments to your boss in your annual appraisal. The average person puts close to two thousand hours of effort every year at their workplace. When I asked some of the people how many hours they put into filling in their appraisal forms, the answer was in a low single digit, and some of them shockingly pegged it at less than one.

Appraisals are not just another corporate exercise that you should do just for the sake of doing it. It is an opportunity and possibly the only one where you are required to sell the brand 'you' and when you can showcase what you have done throughout the year. If you do not take this exercise seriously, you can be certain that your boss won't either, and rightly so. If you don't have anything significant to showcase, you cannot blame others for not seeing it. Spend time collecting information about all the great work you have done, all the endorsements you have received. Don't wait for the appraisal cycle, do it on an ongoing basis. It's hard to remember finer details of things that happened even a month ago, forget about a year. Make sure that you have articulated the situation, the solution, your role, tactical benefits, and strategic benefits of the work you have done and substantiate it with testimonials. Make it difficult to refute. Make it idiot proof.

Keep in mind, appraisals and promotions are one of the most politically charged exercises in any organization, regardless of what your management tells you. If you lose your guard during this time of the year, it can make a serious dent in the year-long effort you put into build your visibility. As they say, the last leg is the toughest.

As the annual appraisal cycle approaches, you will see a lot of opportunists raising their heads. Suddenly everyone will turn into hard and efficient workers ready to deliver more and more for their bosses. They will try to create what is called a recency effect. This is the time when you need to up your selling efforts. Keep your strong proponents warm. Spend some time meeting the influential people who are expected to present their opinion against you and see if you can win a few of them over, but above all spend a good amount of your energy on winning over people who seem to be undecided on whether to vote for or against you. Opportunists can easily influence these unsuspecting people and can sway the momentum away from you. It all comes back to selling and selling at the right time. Win that recency effect. Keep in mind your year-long investment in your visibility beats any opportunists' few days of efforts any day and by miles, you just have to make sure that it remains fresh in people's mind.

The Word of Caution

Whatever way you choose to brand yourself, always use facts to convey the message. This is the only way to safeguard the message and the messenger, whether it is you or someone else. You cannot completely eliminate the subjectivity of the message, but try to keep it at a minimum. There will always be people who will try to tweak or misrepresent the meaning of the message, but it's hard to refute the facts. People think twice about distorting the facts unless they are desperate enough to put their credibility on the line.

Do not try to take credit for something that you did not do. In fact, help others get credit for their work if they are not able to stand up for themselves. This is the most guaranteed way of earning loyalties, and you should take all you can get. It adds extra pounds to your visibility.

Be a pleasant person, easy to talk to, easy to hang out with. If people can't buy you as a person, they will never buy you as a product.

There is an important tip to be shared at this point. At any stage while you are executing the strategies suggested in this book, if you happen to make a mistake, shrug it off and move on. You do not have to walk a tightrope all the time. Performance pressure takes a toll on even the best. Accept that you are human, learn from what happened and move on. Keep in mind your path to visibility will not be up, up, and up; it will be few ups and many downs and then up and away! Don't let the downs intimidate you; they are the pathways to ups. Without a down, there is no up—and that, I think, is pretty much true for anything in life, not just visibility.

So what are you waiting for? Go out and eat that forbidden fruit of selling, for the forbidden fruit is the sweetest!

10- MOTHER'S RECIPE

Whenever the old generation hands over the reins of society to the younger and dynamic new generation, changes are bound to happen. People learn new ways of doing basic things and intellectuals find better ways of doing complicated things. A new wisdom is found, and that is how society moves forward. But there are still some things that have remained unchanged over time. These things have withstood the test of time.

For the species for which the only constant thing is change, the things that have stood their ground warrant some merit. This is the wisdom that was passed from your parents to you and from theirs to them and will, in all probability, be passed from you to your kids. This chapter is dedicated to all those timeless lessons.

To Fight or To Not Fight

Not everybody who dares you to fight is worth fighting. If you have to take away one thing from this book, this would be it.

The easiest way to break someone's composure and rhythm is to engage them in an ugly fight and challenge their ego. By doing so, one can be sure to ruin someone's momentum. People who do not want you to get ahead of them know this well and will use it time and again to slow you down. Sometimes it will be apparent, at other occasions, it will be disguised in various layers of pseudo professionalism or quirky mannerisms. You will have to learn to choose your battles. The biggest determination that you have to make before engaging in a conflict is to know what is at stake, both for you and your opponent. An objective assessment of this question itself will put things in perspective. More often than not you will find that the underlying argument is inconsequential, and it is just the ego that is flaring things up. Immediately withdraw from the situation and try to find the company of positive people.

Even if it comes to the point where you see that the stakes are too high and you need to sort things out, an argument is the last option you want to try. Gather all the facts about the situation and discuss it with someone you trust, someone who is not emotionally invested in the situation. It will help you put things in perspective, and rather than arguing, you can discuss facts. Make sure the discussion is focused on the problem and not the individual. This is a definite way to earn respect from your opponent, even if it is just a small amount. He still won't lose ground to you, but you have called upon his rational side, and though he is still fighting you, you have already got his conscience on your side. Now he has two battles to fight, one with you and another with his conscience.

The other trick that will often be played by your opponent is dragging the fight to a lower and lower and lower level. If you have to fight, fight when the competition is for raising the bar, not when the test is how low you can go. The moment you get into the war of getting low, there is only one way it can end, by creating a dent in your reputation. The scars it will leave and will be everlasting. It is not worth it.

No Visibility for Self-respect

Never compromise your self-respect and values to please someone for short-term benefits. You might see some people getting short-term benefits by compromising their values, but in the long run, they will end up being sidelined. Once people see that you do not have respect for yourself, they will not hesitate for a moment to kick you around the next time they get a chance. Visibility at the cost of your self-respect and values is not worth it.

You Don't Fail Until...

I was once sitting for a job interview and the interviewer asked me, have you ever failed? Without thinking a moment, I said, 'No'. As any interviewer would do, he said, 'You would be the first, who didn't'. Later after we got into the rational discussion, I convinced him that what he is referring to as failures are the mistakes that made me learn and helped me become a better person. It is not failing if you get up and fight again, and that is what I have always done. I've gotten up and fought again, and that is what we have always been told to do by our forefathers—get up and fight again.

Learn to Let Go

Learn to let go of certain things. There will be a time when you will realize that the reward for doing something is not worth the effort that you will put into achieving it or sometimes that it is not even achievable. When you realize that, be strong enough to pull back and let it go. You can still walk with your head high knowing that you did the best you could and that the effort was not worth it, but you can only do that after you have tried your best. Challenge yourself to do big things, but be wise enough to accept when it is time to let go.

What Is an Opinion?

Bill Bullard, a famous US Navy admiral, once said that opinion is really the lowest form of human knowledge. It requires no accountability, no understanding. These two lines actually sum up all there is to say about opinion. When you embark on a journey to achieve something, you will hear people providing you all sorts of unsolicited advice, which, more often than not, is their opinion about things. You have to be careful to filter knowledge from opinion. Sometimes it is just a matter of challenging one's thought to see whether he really understands what he is saying. In any case, do not seek the universe's approval if you want to do something. The only person who needs to approve what you want to do is you. You cannot make the entire world happy, so don't even try.

Introspect

Introspection is the biggest form of assessment. Every day spend some time looking back at the decision that you took, how it has impacted people around you, what you could have done better, and given a chance to do it again, what you would do differently. If you get into the habit of doing this every day, it is worth the teachings of a thousand saints and a thousand books. Be answerable to yourself each day.

Three Is a Crowd—Tell Them

Did you notice that in any typical organization, the process for buying something involves multiple departments: the user, who will use the product or service being purchased; the procurement department, which will negotiate and place the order with the vendor; and accounts payable, which will pay for the order. Did you ever wonder, why they need to have so many entities involved in a simple buying process? Why can't the user negotiate and place the order and then pay for it? It is to avoid fraud. Knowing that many people are aware of the transaction prevents people from doing fraud. You can use this age-old trick to save your credit as well. When you do something that you want to be credited for, make sure at least three or four different people know about it. There are people everywhere who will jump at the chance of taking credit for someone else's hard work. Knowing that your contribution is a publicly known fact becomes a big deterrent for anyone to rip you of the credit that you deserve.

Don't Explain Yourself to Everyone

The rationale around a lot of things you will do to get more visibility would be easily explainable in the context of things, but it is sometimes hard to explain to someone who is not as close to the situation. It is impossible and too painstaking to explain yourself to everyone. Every minute that you waste trying to explain is a minute you could have used for something better. That's not to say that you should not try to explain things to people who matter, but at the same time, you should be prepared for collateral damage. You will not be able to justify yourself to everyone. Some relationships will turn sour in the process, and some bridges will be burned. Rest assured, given a choice, the people who are expecting you to explain yourself will swap positions with you in a jiffy without owing any explanation to you. You need to make sure that you are investing your time explaining things to the people who matter.

How to Deliver the Bad News

People have short attention spans. They forget the details of an event but remember the emotion that they are left with. They start relating that emotion with the associated person. For this subconscious reason, as much as you can, try to distance yourself from bad news. If bad news needs to be delivered, try to make it indirect, or if you absolutely have to be the one to deliver the bad news, try to make yourself as abstract as possible. If possible, make every effort so that people do not recall a bad experience and your face in the same thought. If possible, try to deliver the news in an email, or if it has to be in person, dress conservatively so as to reduce the impact of your presence. This is all, of course, if you are just the news bearer. If you are the one who caused the bad news, go in with a solution to fix the problem.

What's on Their Minds?

It takes two to make a relationship, but it takes one to betray. There is no grief if both are faithful or both are disloyal, the grief is when the feeling is not mutual. The same concept applies to workplace relationships. Whether you consider someone a friend, a colleague, or competition, the feeling has to be mutual, or one of you will get hurt. Don't get too entangled on what you feel about someone; also invest time in finding out what they feel about you.

When in Crisis, Mean Business

When you are thrown into the fire and are in charge of fixing things in a short amount of time, immediately establish your authority and set rules of engagement with the team. In an ideal world, I would have asked you to take some time to get to know people and then decide what will work best, but the longer you wait, more the damage will happen, and your management might start losing patience. If there is limited time to resolve a crisis situation, there is only one certain way: establish your authority and let people know you mean business. Shuffle people around if you have to; let people go if you need to.

Measure-Measure-Measure Results

When you put a lot of effort into something, you tend to be emotionally invested in it. It is easy to get carried away and lose sight of the results the effort was supposed to yield. There is only one measure that tells you whether your efforts are in the right direction, and that measure is results. Every other way of measuring the output of your effort is a way to fool yourself into believing that you are doing a great job. When self-evaluating your efforts, make sure that you define the expected results before you even start putting in the efforts. If possible, write down the expected end result on a piece of paper and keep it safe. This will help you avoid the temptation to change your own expectations later and to trick yourself into believing that your efforts were successful. This also helps you decide whether you need to seek help to get the desired results or set more realistic objectives.

Above all, life is what you make out of it. No riches in this world can make you happy if you don't know how to enjoy the biggest gift of nature called life. Love it and live it to the fullest—for your kids, for your family, and most importantly for yourself. A happy heart cannot make another person sad, and a sad one cannot make another person happy.

These are some age-old lessons that have proven themselves time and again. Parents have told them to their children, by teachers have told them to their students, and now I am telling them to you. Use them and live a blissful life.

www.ingramcontent.com/pod-product-compliance
Lightning Source LLC
Chambersburg PA
CBHW021813170526
45157CB00007B/2572